SS-Sturmbannführer
Ernst August Krag

SS-Sturmbannführer
ERNST AUGUST KRAG
Träger des
Ritterkreuzes mit Eichenlaub

Kommandeur
SS-Sturmgeschützabteilung 2
SS-Panzer-Aufklärungsabteilung 2

"Das Reich"

by

Mark C. Yerger

Title page illustration: Jen Hayes

Schiffer Military History
Atglen, PA

ACKNOWLEDGMENTS

My thanks to the following for their help and advice:
Otto Baum
Leslie DiNizo
Jen Hayes
Ernst August Krag
Karl Kreutz
Fritz Langanke
Jess T. Lukens
John P. Moore
Phil A. Nix
Ruth Sommers
Frank Weaver
Otto Weidinger

and

Truppenkameradschaft "DF"

DEDICATION

To

Mrs. Luise Krag

Book Design by Mark C. Yerger & Robert Biondi.

Library of Congress Catalog Number: 95-73087

Printed in the United States of America.
ISBN: 0-7643-0049-0

We are interested in hearing from authors with book ideas on related topics.

Published by Schiffer Publishing Ltd.
77 Lower Valley Road
Atglen, PA 19310
Please write for a free catalog.
This book may be purchased from the publisher.
Please include $2.95 postage.
Try your bookstore first.

FOREWORD

The American historian Mark C. Yerger, with whom I have been in continuous contact for many years, is especially deserving of gratitude for his continuing efforts to produce biographies of highly decorated members of the former Waffen-SS.

It is a special pleasure for me to honor his request by writing this foreword to the biography of Ernst August Krag. I have known Ernst August Krag since the beginning of his military career in 1936 at Arolsen with the 5th company "Germania." At that time I was an SS-Untersturmführer and platoon leader in the same unit. Together, in 1938, we were both transferred to Klagenfurt, Austria and to the training cadre of Regiment "Der Führer." There our ways parted as I was again transferred. It was only in the summer of 1944 that we met again in France.

In the interim he had become commander of the Aufklärungsabteilung (reconnaissance detachment) of "Das Reich." I personally led this division in union with the division "Götz von Berlichingen" until October 1944 when I transferred to other duties.

With Ernst August Krag the author honors, with good reason, one of the many outstanding soldiers from all ranks within the elite Waffen-SS troops. These were not only commanders, they were true leaders of their soldiers in all situations and, without consideration of their own lives, were always ready to do the same as required of the men they led.

This personal preparedness empowered the troops to achieve the enormous performances required of them at all fronts during this mighty war; and is now respectfully recognized by all of their former enemies. It was their belief in their Fatherland that inspired these men.

Otto Baum
Hechingen-Stetten
1995

INTRODUCTION

This is my fourth biography of a Waffen-SS Ritterkreuzträger (Knight's Cross holder) and as with my previous studies, I endeavor to explain the career of a professional military officer using official records in combination with personal recollections. The career officers of the former Waffen-SS came from all walks of life and entered a new period of military development that allowed an individual to advance on the basis of performance alone compared to the other, more class-structured arms of service existing in the same time period. Ernst August Krag was of the group that benefited from the complete pre-war training system developed under Paul Hausser's supervision, and he became among the most decorated and respected reconnaissance detachment commanders. Allowing myself the input of my personal opinion based on years of correspondence and meeting him, I have found him only concerned with recording his former service's chronicle and very modest as to his own place in history. His contributions to research historians and his own writing verify the first statement while numerous veterans have confirmed the latter. His bravery in the field is proven by his award of the Oakleaves to the Knight's Cross and Wound Badge in Gold; his prowess in battle proven by his place within the official history of the 2.SS-Panzer-Division "Das Reich." The respect he generated among his fellow soldiers remains today, half a century after the Second World War.

Mark C. Yerger
Lancaster, 1996

ERNST AUGUST KRAG

Born in Wiesbaden-Erbenheim on February 20, 1915, Ernst August Krag volunteered for service in the SS-Verfügungstruppe (SS Special Purpose Troops) in May 1935. Assigned to 5./"Germania" (5th Company of Regiment "Germania") for his basic training, he was promoted to SS-Sturmmann (corporal) 7 months later. Krag would spend his entire career assigned to the eventual "Das Reich" division or one of its predecessor sub-components.

After two years of service with "Germania," Krag volunteered for paratroop training at the Luftwaffe Fallschirmspringerschule (paratroop school) in Stendal beginning in May 1937. Taking the course that lasted until July 25, 1937 along with recruits of the 3rd company of Regiment "Hermann Göring," Krag successfully completed the training and participated in six live jumps that qualified him to wear the Luftwaffe Paratrooper Badge. Following graduation from this training, Krag returned to 5./"Germania" for the remaining months of 1937.

When the 3rd regiment of the SS-Verfügungstruppe was established in the spring of 1938 under SS-Standartenführer (colonel) Georg Keppler, Krag transferred to the new SS-Standarte 3 (the eventual Regiment "Der Führer") and was posted to the Klagenfurt-based 9.Kompanie (9th company), a component of SS-Sturmbannführer (Major) Hilmar Wäckerle's III.Bataillon (3rd battalion). Krag and others served as the trained cadre of this unit that would obtain most of its recruits from Austria. At this new assignment came a promotion to SS-Unterscharführer (sergeant) on July 1, 1938.

The military school system to train qualified officer candidates for the SS-Verfügungstruppe was fully established by the time Krag was selected to attend the course commencing November 1, 1938 at the Bad Tölz facility. This was the final full length pre-war course and lasted until August 22, 1939 under the supervision of SS-Standartenführer Werner Freiherr von Schele.[1] Krag was trained for several more months before his promotion to SS-Junker on January 15, 1939. Due to the traditional dates of commissioning officers, Krag's promotion to SS-Untersturmführer (2nd lieutenant) became effective on November 9, 1939.

A combination of various specialty units of the SS-Verfügungstruppe into a field division was an eventuality already foreseen upon establishing the first units in 1935. The final unit to be created and initially assigned to the division that became "Das Reich" was the artillery contingent. This regiment was formed in June 1939 at the Heeres-Artillerie-Schule (Army Artillery School) Jüterbog and was commanded by SS-Obersturmbannführer (lieutenant colonel) Peter Hansen.[2] Krag and other recent cadets from SS-Junkerschulen (SS Officer Schools) Bad Tölz and Braunschweig were assigned to the regiment and completed the first artillery officer candidate course from August 23 to October 17, 1939.

[1] Schele had been an instructor at Junkerschule Braunschweig before transferring to Bad Tölz. He retired by 1942 with the rank of SS-Oberführer after serving on the staff of SS-Oberabschnitt "Süd," having been promoted to his last rank on February 15, 1940

[2] Lacking an experienced artillery commander, Hansen transferred to the SS/VT from the Army with the rank of SS-Obersturmbannführer effective June 1, 1939. He had been in command of s.Artillerie Abteilung (heavy artillery detachment) 50 (14.Infanterie Division). Hansen left the Division in September 1941, serving in various artillery-related staff positions in the SS-Führungshauptamt until February 1943. For the remainder of the war he served in various staff and command assignments, ending the war as Chief of Staff, XVIII.SS-Armee-Korps (18th SS Army Corps) and was promoted to SS-Brigadeführer (Lt. General) on January 30, 1942.

Each Abteilung (detachment) of the Regiment contained three Batterien (batteries) along with a leichte Artillerie Kolonne (light artillery column) for each Abteilung. Each Batterie had a Beobachtungsoffizier (observation officer) and a Batterie Offizier (battery or fire control officer) commanded by a Batterie Chef (battery commander). Assigned to SS-Obersturmbannführer Herbert Gille's 1st detachment, Krag became the Batterie Offizier of 3rd battery upon final completion of the officer candidate course.[3]

During mid-October 1939 the regiment moved to Pilsen and was incorporated into the new SS-V.T.-Division (mot) (SS Special Troop Division [motorized]) under Paul Hausser's leadership. Hausser had established the SS-Junkerschule "Braunschweig" and was the senior SS officer most responsible for the development of the Waffen-SS. This single most influential officer upon Krag, as far as his career was concerned, would lead the division until wounded in October 1941.[4]

While the division continued its development and acquainted itself with operating as a single field unit, Krag's specialized instruction continued. Along with the other junior officers of the Artillery Regiment, he attended a signal communications course at the Heeres-Nachrichtenschule Halle (Army Signals School Halle) from early January to February 11, 1940. Returning to his unit, Krag was made adjutant of 1st detachment, serving in this capacity for the division's campaigns against the western powers and was awarded the Iron Cross 2nd class on July 25, 1940. During the summer months the division was stationed in Holland for coastal defense duties and continued its own training curriculum.

Krag officially remained detachment adjutant until the end of 1940. Beginning in the middle of September 1940, he served as a Zugführer (platoon leader) in the 1.Unterführerlehrbatterie (NCO training battery) which trained non-commissioned officers in Amersfoort, Holland. Krag served in this capacity and led these NCO aspirants until the second week of December 1940.

During April 1940, a heavy artillery detachment had become operational within the regiment and Krag was reassigned to it in the spring of 1941 as battery leader of 11th battery.[5] The IV.(s) Abteilung (4th [heavy] detachment) was equipped with 15cm long range weapons under the command of SS-Hauptsturmführer (captain) Karl Kreutz.[6] Krag held this position during the brief Yugoslavian campaign and on April 20, 1941 was promoted to SS-Obersturmführer (1st Lieutenant). Following this, the division prepared for the upcoming offensive in Russia, where Krag would

---

[3] When the Regiment was formed, Gille became initial commander of I.Abteilung, having previously commanded II./Germania. In December 1940 he left the Division to take command of the Artillerie Regiment of the new "Germania" Division (later retitled "Wiking"). He took command of this Division on May 1, 1943 and became IV.SS-Panzer-Korps Commander on July 20, 1944. Gille won the German Cross in Gold (February 28, 1942) and Knight's Cross (October 8, 1942) as Artillerie Regimentskommandeur. As a divisional commander he was awarded the Oakleaves (November 1, 1943), Swords (February 20, 1944), and Diamonds (April 20, 1944) to his Knight's Cross. His last promotion, to SS-Obergruppenführer, became effective November 9, 1944.

[4] See "SS-Oberst-Gruppenführer Paul Hausser" by Mark C. Yerger for the career of the senior Waffen-SS commander.

[5] The heavy detachment was first designated V.Abteilung while the first formed IV.Abteilung was established for the "Leibstandarte" under the Division's supervision. In its early form under SS-Sturmbannführer Karl Rees, the heavy unit Batterien were numbered 13, 14 and 15. After its Abteilung number changed, the Batterien were numbered 10, 11 and 12.

[6] Kreutz commanded both 2.Batterie (June 1939 to February 1941) and 6.Batterie (February to April 1941) before taking command of IV.Abteilung in April 1941. As Abteilungskommandeur he won the German Cross in Gold on December 17, 1943. Taking command of the entire Artillerie Regiment in March 1943, he won both the Knight's Cross (September 5, 1944) and the Oakleaves (May 6, 1945) for this command. He twice commanded "Das Reich" (January 20, 1945 to February 4, 1945 and April 18, 1945 until the end of the war). He was promoted to SS-Standartenführer on April 20, 1944.

command 5th battery during the first months of fighting under the commander of 2nd detachment, SS-Sturmbannführer Max Wunder.

The incredible pace of the first months of Barbarossa imposed heavy combat as well as tactical stress for all members of the division, as units often moved faster than their support elements, a situation especially felt by the heavy weapon units such as the Artillery Regiment. On July 27, 1941, Krag was awarded the Iron Cross 1st class for his efforts in the opening phase of the campaign.

During the heavy fighting for Jelnja the sub-units of the division began to suffer losses faster than replacements could be obtained. As the battles moved towards central Russia, staff batteries were incorporated as temporary replacements. Under-equipped with regard to winter clothing and other critically needed supplies, the division fought as the main offensive spearhead in the attempt to capture Moscow. The hardships Krag and the other men of the division faced in the first Soviet winter can only be understood by the men who were actually there. The losses in junior officers were severe due to their characteristic of leading the troops under their command from the front of the fighting. When "Reich" moved to its new location SW of Sytschevka in December 1941, Krag was transferred to SS-Hauptsturmführer (captain) Wilhelm Kment's Aufklärungsabteilung (reconnaissance detachment) to take command of 2.Kompanie.[7]

While fighting at Sytschevka alongside elements of the Army 1.Panzer-Division, Krag was severely wounded on January 23, 1942. In the night of January 23rd during bitter cold and a heavy snowfall, strong Russian forces broke through the weakly held protective lines of the Aufklärungsabteilung and pushed forward to the Abteilung command post. In hand-to-hand fighting the enemy was thrown back with heavy casualties on both sides. After initial medical treatment Krag was evacuated to the field hospital in Lötzen/East Prussia and later moved to a hospital in Mainz to recover. In the following few months the majority of the division would withdraw to Fallingbostel for a complete rest and refit, leaving behind temporarily a small Kampfgruppe (battle group) led by the former 1.Generalstabsoffizier (1st General Staff Officer or Ia) of the division, SS-Standartenführer Werner Ostendorff.

During Krag's recovery, SS-Gruppenführer (major general) Georg Keppler took command of the Division, undertaking leadership for the single largest expansion of the unit beginning April 1, 1942. When this refitting completed, the new divisional title would be, effective November 9, 1942, SS-Panzer-Grenadier-Division "Das Reich."[8] Following his recovery Krag returned to the Artillery Regiment on May 1, 1942.[9] With his organizational abilities proven as a detachment adjutant and combat performance a matter of regimental record, he was selected as regimental

---

[7] Position confirmed by Soldbuch entry, copy courtesy Herr Krag. For Wilhelm Kment's career see "Otto Weidinger, Knights Cross with Oakleaves and Swords," footnote 16.

[8] The Division had seven titles during its history: October 10, 1939 to April 1, 1940 SS-V.T.-Division (mot), April 1, 1940 to November 30, 1940 SS-V.-Division, December 1, 1940 to January 27, 1941 SS-Division "Deutschland," January 28, 1941 to May 1942 SS-Division "Reich," May 1942 to November 9, 1942 SS-Division "Das Reich," November 9, 1942 to January 1944 SS-Panzer-Grenadier-Division "Das Reich," and January 1944 to the end of the war 2.SS-Panzer-Grenadier-Division "Das Reich." In those dates which do not agree with previous texts, the author has taken dates from SS-FHA directives signed by Himmler from National Archives Records Group T-175. Some dates were recorded at a later time in the Division Kriegstagebuch (War Diary or KTB).

[9] SS-Führungshauptamt, Kommandoamt der Waffen-SS, IIa Az:21c 16/Br./FHu. "Personalverfügung."

adjutant by new artillery regiment commander SS-Standartenführer Kurt Brasack.[10] This would be his last assignment within the unit he had served with since being commissioned.

In his new assignment, Krag assisted in the rebuilding of large portions of the regiment's losses incurred the previous year. Three medium batteries and two of heavy caliber were completely rebuilt, as well as several staff batteries.[11] In addition, the unit prepared for the acceptance of self-propelled artillery that became incorporated into 1st detachment and greatly add to the regiment's offensive capability. From the close combats the previous year, Krag was awarded the Infanterie-Sturmabzeichen (Infantry Assault Badge) on July 14, 1942 and the Ostmedaille (Eastern Front Medal) on August 3, 1942. During this lengthy expansion, the Division also finally obtained armor.

A Panzer Abteilung (tank detachment) formed in April 1942 and, simultaneously with this unit being expanded to a Panzer Regiment, a Sturmgeschützabteilung (assault gun detachment) was also added to the division in October 1942.[12] Led by the former commander of III./"Deutschland," SS-Hauptsturmführer Walter Kniep, the primary officers and composition of the newly formed unit were as follows:

Commander	SS-Hauptsturmführer Walter Kniep
Adjutant	SS-Untersturmführer d.R. Heinrich Köhler
Ordnance Officer:	SS-Untersturmführer Hartmut Braun
Medical Officer	SS-Obersturmführer Dr. Fritz Sedlaczek
Administration Officer:	SS-Obersturmführer Fritz Dietrich
Technical Officer for Vehicles:	SS-Obersturmführer Anton Beinl
Technical Officer for Weapons:	SS-Untersturmführer Fritz Brune
Staff Battery Chief	SS-Obersturmführer Friedrich Wilhelm Graun
1st Battery Commander:	SS-Obersturmführer Eberhard Telkamp[13]
2nd Battery Commander:	SS-Obersturmführer Ernst August Krag
3rd Battery Commander:	SS-Obersturmführer Siegfried Kepp[14]

[10] Brasack transferred from command of I./Artillerie Regiment "Wiking" having began his career with command of I./Artillerie Regiment "Totenkopf." When Herbert Vahl was wounded in March 1943 Brasack assumed command of the division, having commanded the Artillerie Regiment since January 1942. As Division Commander, Brasack signed Krag's German Cross in Gold recommendation. After leaving the Division he served as Nachschubkommandeur der Waffen-SS und Polizei "Ostland" and ended the war as Arko (senior artillery commander) IV.SS-Panzer-Korps. Promoted SS-Brigadeführer on January 1, 1945, he was awarded the German Cross in Gold on October 19, 1944 while commanding SS-Artillerie-Regiment 54.

[11] SS-FHA Org.Tgb.Nr.66/42 g.Kdos. "Gliederung der SS-Div. 'Reich'" dated March 5, 1942.

[12] SS-Führungshauptamt Kdo. Amt.d.Waffen-SS, Org.Tgb.Nr.476/42g.Kdos. "Aufstellung von Panzer-und Sturmgeschützeinheiten für das SS-Panzer-Regiment 2, für die Sturmgeschütz Abteilung 2 der SS-Division 'Das Reich'" dated October 14, 1942.

[13] Awarded the German Cross in Gold on February 28, 1942 while a Sturmgeschütz commander in the single Batterie, which existed in 1941 before the later Sturmgeschützabteilung was formed, subordinated to the Artillerie Regiment. It was disbanded in early 1942 before the Abteilung was established due to attrition. He left the division to become a Panzer-Abteilungskommandeur in the 9.SS-Panzer-Division "Hohenstaufen" where he won the Knight's Cross on August 23, 1944. He later commanded the unit's Panzer Regiment and ended the war as an SS-Obersturmbannführer. In the first months after transferring he commanded the Sturmgeschützabteilung of the 9.SS-Panzer-Division "Hohenstaufen."

[14] Kepp entered the SS/VT with the Nachrichtenabteilung (signals detachment) SS/VT in 1937. He was posted to the Division after attending Junkerschule "Braunschweig" in 1940 and was awarded the German Cross in Gold on April 9, 1943 as commander of 3./Sturmgeschützabteilung. After leaving the Division he served in positions with various Sturmgeschütz training and replacement units as well as instructing at SS-Sturmgeschütz-Schule "Janowitz." In that later teaching position he was promoted to SS-Sturmbannführer on January 1, 1945.

Each Batterie contained seven weapons at initial normal strength for a total of 28 weapons including the commander's vehicle. As divided into three Züge (platoons), Krag's Zugführer (platoon leaders) were SS-Untersturmführer Steffen Chemnitz, SS-Untersturmführer August Hoffmann, and SS-Untersturmführer Otto Enderle. Upon assuming his new command, Krag left for Jüterbog to attend a class for Sturmgeschütze with the facility's Lehrstab (teaching staff) from November 8th to December 15, 1942.

The detachment obtained its Sdkfz 141s, equipped with 7.5cm weapons, at the Debica training area in Poland, and quickly became familiar with their new mounts prior to departure for Russia in January 1943. In January, commander Kniep, obviously impressed with Krag's performance of his duties in only three months, recommended him for promotion to the rank of SS-Hauptsturmführer.

"Das Reich" and "Leibstandarte" formed SS-Panzer-Korps (SS Armored Corps) under the command of Paul Hausser when it left for Russia in early January 1943. Joined the following month by "Totenkopf," all three would spend the majority of 1943 in almost constant combat with the initial engagements commencing almost immediately upon their arrival.

On February 15, 1943, Krag led his Batterie along with 3./Pionier Bataillon (3rd company of the engineer battalion) and 5./"Der Führer" (5th company of Regiment "Der Führer") in stiff combat along the road connecting Kulnitschi and Terekhoff, destroying large quantities of material and fulfilling his assigned objectives. Typically acknowledging the performance of his subordinates, his report of the combat would later form a partial basis of a German Cross in Gold being awarded to one of his Sturmgeschütz commanders, SS-Unterscharführer Alfred Idel.[15]

Later in February, "Das Reich" was required to capture several bridges in their drive to capture Pawlograd. The fighting for these three rail bridges was a prerequisite for the Division to continue the advance towards the town that lay on the Samara River. II./"Der Führer," under SS-Obersturmbannführer Silvester Stadler's command, was ordered to capture all three crossing points.[16]

"On February 21, 1943, II./'Der Führer' was ordered to form and hold a bridgehead at Pawlograd, crossing over three bridges. The first could be taken by a direct frontal attack. Then enemy resistance stiffened, and it looked as if the attack would come to a standstill, mainly as further advance by the assault guns seemed impossible due to severe anti-tank fire.

"Upon his own decision, SS-Obersturmführer Krag attacked with his battery over the first bridge, destroying three anti-tank guns and several machine gun positions. By this action our infantry could make progress over the 2nd and 3rd bridges. Krag therefore supported the attack and had a leading role in the battalion's success, as this was a condition for the division's further advance."[17]

Two days later the division had moved slightly north toward Werbki in its northerly attack toward Losowaja. At this time a Soviet counterattack attempted to retake Pawlograd.

15 "Vorschlagliste für die Verleihung des Deutschen Kreuzes in Gold" dated March 20, 1943. Idel transferred to the Sturmgeschützabteilung from 5./"Der Führer" and was awarded his German Cross in Gold on April 15, 1943 as an SS-Unterscharführer and Geschützführer (vehicle commander).

16 For Silvester Stadler's career see "Otto Weidinger, Knight's Cross with Oakleaves and Swords," footnote 34.

17 "Begründung und Stellungnahme des Zwischenvorgesetzten" for the German Cross in Gold dated March 13, 1943 and signed by Kniep.

"On February 23, 1943, II./'Der Führer' defended Pawlograd from the north. During the night the enemy broke through with 10 tanks. The attack was repulsed, and in the morning 7./'Der Führer' and 2./Sturmgeschützabteilung, under the command of SS-Obersturmführer Krag, launched a counterattack. Under the skilled command of SS-Obersturmführer Krag's support of the attack, one anti-tank gun and six machine gun positions were destroyed. Due to this, 7./'Der Führer' could accomplish its mission without losses of their own, having destroyed 272 Russian troops."[18]

After firmly securing Pawlograd's defensive perimeter, the division attacked Werbki that was the next Soviet strongpoint. The severity of combat for the town is exemplified in that the recording of the engagement in Krag's Soldbuch became combat credit toward an eventual award of the Close Combat Clasp.

"Krag's Batterie was seconded to II./'Deutschland' for the attack on Werbki. The first target was the bridge near the southwest entrance of the town. The basic idea was to take that bridge in a surprise assault. Krag's battery pushed forward for that purpose as quickly as possible, carrying along a group of engineers as well as members of 6./'Deutschland.' However, the bridge had been mined and was ready to be blown up. Immediately after arriving at the bridge that the enemy had successfully destroyed, SS-Obersturmführer Krag opened fire on the heavy armor of the enemy. Their crews left the vehicles in hasty flight. We can thank Krag's battery for making it possible for our infantry to occupy the southwest entry and southern outskirts of Werbki without further difficulties. This area had been fortified strongly with anti-tank weapons and a few tanks. Our forces were able to capture these weapons of the enemy.

"After SS-Obersturmführer Krag had battled the enemy's heavy weapons, he succeeded in reaching Werbki west of the destroyed bridge over the Samara river. He then pushed on immediately with his battery from the southwest entry of the town to its northwest exit. All this time his guns were without protection from the infantry. It was there that Krag made first contact with the leading armored elements of the SS-Division 'Totenkopf.' "[19]

After securing Werbki, the division continued its northerly advance to Losowaja, which lay along the Bratal river. These attacks in the final week of February 1943 found Krag's Batterie in support of the division's Kradschützen Bataillon (motorcycle battalion), under the command of SS-Sturmbannführer Jakob Fick.[20] While supporting the 3.Kompanie of Fick's command, Krag noticed an attack by Soviet armor on troops of SS-Obersturmbannführer Silvester Stadler's II./"Der Führer."

[18] ibid.

[19] ibid.

[20] The Kradschützen-Bataillon was formed in February, 1941 and became the I.Bataillon of Regiment "Langemarck" when this unit was formed in May, 1942. It was still referred to within the Division as the Kradschützen-Bataillon. In April 1943 "Langemarck" was dissolved and used to strengthen other units including the Aufklärungsabteilung. Fick took command of the Bataillon in May, 1942 and was awarded the Knight's Cross on April 23, 1943 for his leadership of the Bataillon. In April, 1943 he became leader of the Aufklärungsabteilung where he stayed until transfer to the 17.SS-Panzer-Grenadier-Division "Götz von Berlichingen" as commander of SS-Panzer-Grenadier-Regiment 38. He ended the war, having briefly commanded this later division, with the rank of SS-Standartenführer. He left "Das Reich" in August, 1943 having served with the Division and the SS/VT since 1934.

"On February 26th, 1943, II./'Der Führer' attacked Losowaja. During that preparation the enemy launched a counterattack, supported by three T-34s, which put II./'Der Führer' in a somewhat critical situation and pinned it down. SS-Obersturmführer Krag, with two guns in the neighboring sector with the Kradschützen-Bataillon, observed this situation and destroyed two of the tanks and thus saved the situation. After conferring with the commander of the Kradschützen-Bataillon, Krag continued to support the infantry attacks of II./'Der Führer' in an extraordinary manner, destroying nine tanks (T-34) and a similar number of machine gun positions." [21]

The fighting continued into the following day with increased Soviet resistance and counterattacks. By then Krag's Batterie was again supporting the motorcycle infantry of Jakob Fick's command, allowing the town of Losowaja to be permanently secured.

"Krag's Batterie was attached to the Kradschützen-Bataillon on February 27th, 1943. SS-Obersturmführer Krag supported the attack of the Kradschützen-Bataillon on the northwestern district of the Losowaja railway. Here also he contributed significantly to the success of the operation with his spirited assaults." [22]

The division would next take Rasdolje in attacks aimed at the eventual capture of Jefremowka. For these attacks, Krag's Batterie attached to Regiment "Der Führer" while 3.Batterie, now commanded by later Knight's Cross holder Dr. Wolfgang Roehder, was assigned to Regiment "Deutschland."

"Attacking Rasdolje on February 28th, 1943, the 2./Sturmgeschützabteilung, in close cooperation with 5./'Der Führer,' received the order to break through and enter the town. Heavy anti-tank fire supported by several tanks could not stop SS-Obersturmführer Krag's attack. Very skillfully he placed his guns so that in close-range fighting, four T-34s, three anti-tank positions and several machine guns were destroyed. This enabled the attack of 5./'Der Führer' to progress so that the target could be secured." [23]

March began with combats to secure Jefremowka along the Orel river. The fighting had been bitter in the first month of combat and by the end of the first week of March 1943, the Sturmgeschützabteilung had nine vehicles remaining on its Order of Battle.[24] Having secured Rasdolje, Krag and his unit continued as armored support for II./"Der Führer."

"On March 1, 1943, 'Das Reich' made its way from Rasdolje to Jefremowka. Krag and his battery were always with the leading company. They had a leading role in preventing the enemy

---

[21] See footnote 17.

[22] ibid.

[23] ibid..

[24] Otto Weidinger, "Division Das Reich," volume IV, page 70.

from building new defensive positions on the outskirts of Jefremowka. The next day the attack continued by II./'Der Führer' in spite of severe enemy artillery, anti tank, tank fire and mortars and machine guns, but due to these reasons the attack made little progress. SS-Obersturmführer Krag approached with his battery, and due to his excellently chosen positions, he out gunned eight tanks (three T-34s), nine anti tank guns, and numerous machine gun positions. Furthermore, 19 guns were captured, at least 3/4 of them having been destroyed by Krag's battery during the fighting. The successful attack of II./'Der Führer' was mainly the result of Krag and his gun support." [25]

Despite the lack of experience with their vehicles, Krag's men were an equal match for the Russian T-34s, and tactically advantageous situations produced impressive results. Several of the vehicle commanders scored more than 30 tank kills against the Soviets and, as will be seen later, the Sturmgeschützabteilung ended the year with one of the highest ratios of destroyed vehicles per weapon lost within "Das Reich." The combat in the first week of March 1943 would inspire Walter Kniep to recommend that Krag be awarded the German Cross in Gold for his efforts during combat from his arrival in Russia until the eve of the Kharkov battles.[26]

"On March 3, 1943, Krag's battery was still supporting the Kradschützen-Bataillon. At 0600 hours, the Russians launched an attack with 2000 men in the depression of Losovaja and at the height southwest of the town. The enemy was beaten and destroyed in the concentrated fire of all our available weapons. At that time, Krag's battery destroyed an active anti-tank battery of four weapons. The enemy lost at least 200 men killed or wounded through the actions of Krag's weapons.

"On March 7 and 8, 1943, SS-Obersturmführer Krag and his guns supported the attack of III./ 'Der Führer' on Stanaja Vodolaga. In the course of the battle Krag destroyed two anti-tank guns with his assault gun as well as two horse-driven sleds loaded with munitions and supplies. The enemy casualties included at least fifteen dead and twenty wounded." [27]

With severe cold and heavy losses already suffered by the Division, the fierce battles for Kharkov and Bjelgorod were a fight against a determined enemy as well as the elements. With a few newly arrived replacements, Hausser's Korps captured Kharkov in close-range fighting which gave the enemy the tactical advantage. The capture of the city was the largest Waffen-SS victory of the war and the last offensive success against a large city by German ground forces.[28]

The city was in German control by March 14, 1943, and the fighting toward the north of Bjelgorod continued for the following week. In mid-March 1943 the Sturmgeschützabteilung destroyed 14

[25] See footnote 17.

[26] "Vorschlagliste Nr. 1 für die Verleihung des Deutschen Kreuzes in Gold" signed by Kniep on March 13, 1943 and approved by Brasack and Hausser on March 22, 1943.

[27] ibid.

[28] These battles resulted in more awards of the Knight's Cross and German Cross than any other Waffen-SS battle. See Krätschmer "Die Ritterkreuzträger der Waffen-SS" and the official histories of the three units involved.

Russian tanks in cooperation with Regiment "Deutschland" commanded by SS-Standartenführer Heinz Harmel.[29]

When Walter Kniep signed Krag's German Cross in Gold recommendation, he wrote a commentary at the end of his report that gives some insight into Kniep's opinion of Krag as a Batterie Chef:

"SS-Obersturmführer Krag proved to be a brave officer and a fearless, dashing daredevil in every combat action. He led his battery in all battles with great tactical skill and was a model of courage and bravery for his NCOs and men." [30]

On April 9, 1943, the award of the German Cross in Gold was approved for Krag and later presented to him by "Das Reich" divisional commander SS-Gruppenführer Walter Krüger. On April 20, 1943, Kniep's request that Krag be promoted was approved and, effective that date, he attained the rank of SS-Hauptsturmführer.

The Division got a brief refit in the field beginning in April 1943 to prepare for the upcoming summer battles that included the largest armor engagements in history. Replacements brought the Sturmgeschützabteilung to a strength of 33 vehicles at this time.[31] Not only did the division get replacements for its armor units, but it also incorporated T-34s captured at Kharkov into its inventory. [32]

The battles of extreme intensity from July 5-17 were the most geographically compressed armor engagements of the war, and the success of the Sturmgeschützabteilung is best explained with their number of victories and other relative facts, as no war diary of the unit for that period survived. The battles at Kursk involved the best of the Soviet armor units against II.SS-Panzer-Korps that had no superiors within the German Armed Forces. On July 8, 1943, the Abteilung intercepted an attack by 170 Russian armored vehicles, and along with Regiments "Deutschland" and "Der Führer," they destroyed 92 Soviet tanks of which 51 were credited to the Abteilung for the loss of one vehicle. [33] In the period of July 5-17, 1943, the Sturmgeschützabteilung destroyed 129 enemy tanks for the loss of two of their own.[34]

Walter Kniep was awarded the Knight's Cross in recognition for his unit's performance on August 14, 1943, for these July battles. The fact that Kniep selected Krag as his replacement to command the Abteilung attests to Krag's combat performance, confirming and commending both his skill as a tactician as well as his personal bravery. On July 14, Krag was wounded again. He

[29] Otto Weidinger, "Division "Das Reich," Volume IV.

[30] See footnote 26.

[31] II.SS-Panzer-Korps, Ia, Kriegstagbuch Nr.6, entry for July 2, 1943.

[32] Personnel from the Panzerjäger Abteilung and Panzer Regiment were formed into III./Panzer Regiment with those T-34s captured (and some completed that were found in a factory) and added to the Division until maintaining the weapons became impossible. Sources range from 25-33 as the number of the tanks being in inventory at peak strength. Hausser had 6 of them returned to Germany to be used in anti-tank training.

[33] "Vorschlagsliste Nr.17 für die Verleihung des Ritterkreuzes zum Eisernen Kreuz," application for the Knight's Cross for Walter Kniep in recognition for the actions of his command and signed by Walter Krüger on July 31, 1943. Kniep was awarded the Knight's Cross on July 31, 1943 having previously won the first German Cross in Gold awarded to a member of the Division on November 15, 1941.

[34] ibid.

would be wounded yet another time during the Mius river fighting on August 3rd and awarded the Wound Badge in Silver the following day after his command vehicle hit a mine that also wounded the detachment adjutant, Heinrich Köhler.[35]

A Wehrmacht report dated August 27, 1943, credited and congratulated "Das Reich" for the destruction of 1000 enemy tanks in 35 combat days recorded beginning with the March Kharkov battles. In the official history of "Das Reich" these victories are credited as follows: 500 for the Panzer Regiment, 250 for the Sturmgeschützabteilung, and 250 for the Panzer-Grenadier-Regimenter and other units.[36] A normal strength Panzer Abteilung contained four Kompanien with three Züge, each of the latter with five vehicles. The Panzer Regiment had two detachments. The Sturmgeschützabteilung contained three batteries and a staff battery for a total strength of 28 operational assault guns including the command vehicle. They therefore equaled the strength of about two Panzer companies (about 25% the strength of the Panzer Regiment).

On a per unit strength basis, the Sturmgeschützabteilung destroyed *twice as many vehicles* as the Panzer Regiment. These figures, while not intended to lessen the sacrifice of other units, amply show the contribution of Krag and the men of the assault gun detachment.

During August 1943, Krag became temporary commander of the Sturmgeschützabteilung, an appointment made permanent when record keeping in Berlin caught up to events in the field. During this month Walter Kniep returned to Germany for reassignment to the 17.SS-Panzer-Grenadier-Division "Götz von Berlichingen" as the first commander of its tank detachment.

Krag led the Sturmgeschützabteilung in combat for the bridgehead near Saporoshje and was wounded again on October 14, 1943. "Das Reich" continued fighting along the main roads leading to Kiev during late October to mid-November, 1943, when the unit transported to the area around Korostyschew in preparation for the Shitomir battles of December. Despite the extreme losses of the Division, the Abteilung asserted itself well as can be seen by the award of the Knight's Cross to one of Krag's Batterie commanders, Dr. Wolfgang Roehder. A close friend of Krag's and the junior officer who impressed him the most, Roehder would later command the Abteilung at Krag's recommendation.[37]

The Division earned a full rest and refit, and the majority of "Das Reich" left for Germany for rebuilding as a Panzer Division at Fallingbostel. Krag's men left their remaining vehicles with Kampfgruppe (battle group) "Das Reich," and these formed into two companies led by SS-Hauptsturmführer Hans-Joachim Mützelfeldt.[38] The members of this Kampfgruppe returned during March and April of 1944 at which time they were again incorporated into the division.

Krag oversaw the rebuilding of the Sturmgeschützabteilung in the first months of 1944 and was officially made commander on February 20, 1944.[39] He would lead the Abteilung against the

---

[35] Letter to the author from Herr Krag dated November 16, 1986.

[36] Otto Weidinger, "Division Das Reich," volume IV.

[37] Letter to the author from Herr Krag dated November 19, 1985.

[38] Mützelfeld had commanded 3./Flak Abteilung where he won the German Cross in Gold on November 26, 1943. The remaining Sturmgeschütz weapons did well with Kampfgruppe "Das Reich" as evidenced by the German Cross in Gold to Untersturmführer Karl Gerlach (July 2, 1944) and Hauptscharführer Gerhard Hecker (July 2 , 1944) for their actions with the mixed Sturmgeschütz unit attached to the Kampfgruppe.

[39] SS-Führungshauptamt, Amt V/Abt.IIa/Ref.3,Az.21c 16 Lg/Ge Stu.Gesch "Personalverfügung."

allies after D-Day for only a short time before transferring to command the Aufklärungsabteilung, which was also being rebuilt after heavy losses. In April, divisional commander SS-Brigadeführer Heinz Lammerding requested Krag's promotion to SS-Sturmbannführer. This final promotion became effective less than two weeks later on April 20, 1944.

As "Das Reich" moved to engage the allies in June 1944, the tactical problems were far different from Russia. The constant threat of air attack held daylight movement to a minimum due to the possibility of fighter bomber attacks that caused heavy losses throughout the campaign. The lack of fuel and sufficient supplies from Germany added further problems for all units. Losses in combat were severe and Krag was again wounded on July 5, 1944, in the fighting southwest of La-Haye-du-Puits.

During the first week of July 1944, the commander of the Aufklärungsabteilung, SS-Hauptsturmführer Heinrich Wulf, was wounded.[40] Two weeks later Krag signed a final award request for one of his Zugführer, Roland Paul, who among other accomplishments had destroyed 37 Soviet tanks in a six month period the previous summer. A week before signing this request for the German Cross in Gold on July 21, 1944, Krag led Paul and others in an attack with elements of Regiment "Deutschland" in the St. Loieferte area, destroying three Shermans.[41] Krag relinquished his command of the Sturmgeschützabteilung to SS-Hauptsturmführer Dr. Wolfgang Roehder and became the last commander of the Aufklärungsabteilung.[42]

The fighting in Normandy had been bitter from the beginning with many senior officers killed or wounded. Heinz Lammerding was wounded and replaced by Christian Tychsen who had previously commanded the Panzer Regiment. When an American armored spearhead attacked the divisional headquarters at the Trelly crossroads, Tychsen was killed. He was replaced by later Swords to the Knight's Cross winner Otto Baum on July 28, 1944.[43] It would be Baum who would recommend Krag for the Knight's Cross for his actions in the Coutance area during late July 1944.

Krag's new command contained four combat Kompanien (companies) and a support Kompanie. Equipped with a variety of four and eight wheeled armored cars as well as one type of semi-tracked vehicle, the unit was often at the head of the division facing enemy units with superior firepower. Krag's command also contained the famous Schwimmwagen (amphibious vehicle) designed by

[40] Heinrich Wulf transferred from a teaching position at SS-Junkerschule Bad Tölz to Kampfgruppe "Das Reich" and commanded its mixed Aufklärungskompanie. He was recommended for the German Cross in Gold by Lammerding and returned to Germany and assumed command of the Aufklärungsabteilung from Hauptsturmführer Walter Drexler who commanded those parts of the unit already undergoing rebuild. Wulf graduated from Braunschweig in 1938 and was promoted to SS-Sturmbannführer on January 1, 1945 when he was serving with the Panzer-Aufklärungs-Ersatz-Abteilung.

[41] "Vorschlag Nr.4 für die Verleihung des Deutschen Kreuzes in Gold," dated July 21, 1944 and signed by Krag. Paul, an SS-Obersturmführer and Zugführer with 3.Batterie, was awarded the German Cross in Gold on August 28, 1944. By that time the Panzer Regiment had been resupplied by the Sturmgeschützabteilung and Panzerjäger Abteilung and these two units combined. While most officers were from the Sturmgeschützabteilung, their weapons were mostly from the Panzerjäger Abteilung. The application for Paul's German Cross is stamped Stug. Abt. while the document heading page reads Pz.Jg.Abt., thus showing the time period when the Sturmgeschützabteilung became part of the Panzerjäger Abteilung and Krag relinquished his command.

[42] Among the previous commanders were Dr. Wim Brandt (camouflage clothing developer), Hans Mühlenkamp (later Oakleaves winner with "Wiking"), Wilhelm Kment (German Cross in Gold with Kradschützen-Bataillon "Das Reich"), Hans Weiss (Knight's Cross with sSS-Panzer Abteilung 102), Otto Weidinger (Swords to the Knight's Cross as commander of Regiment "Der Führer"), Jakob Fick (Knight's Cross with I./ "Langemarck"), and Heinrich Wulf (see footnote 40).

[43] Tychsen had replaced Lammerding who had been wounded. After Tychsen's capture Baum was given command while at the same time led the 17.SS-Panzer-Grenadier-Division "Götz von Berlichingen." Baum was awarded the Swords to the Knight's Cross for his leadership of "Das Reich" on September 2, 1944. Lammerding returned to command the Division on November 1, 1944 and Baum left to take command of the 16.SS-Panzer-Grenadier-Division "Reichsführer-SS."

Prof. Dr. Ferdinand Porsche. Upon taking command, Krag and the others of the division faced the necessity of evacuating themselves from the Coutance area. During the breakout Krag's Aufklärungsabteilung would fight in conjunction with Regiment "Deutschland," protecting the flank of the Division against the Canadian troops attacking towards Granville.

"When during the night of July 28/29, 1944, the 2.SS-Panzer-Division 'Das Reich' broke through from its encirclement northeast of Avranches toward the southwest to form a new defensive line between Percy and Sourdevall, SS-Sturmbannführer Krag blocked off the already infiltrating enemy in Gavray and thus prevented an attack into the open flank of the division. Being well aware of his own exposed position, Krag acted upon his own responsibility and decision and with his inferior forces won a complete defensive success against a superior strength enemy.

"The brave fight, which SS-Sturmbannführer Krag and his unit dominated, enabled his division and other units of LXXXIV.Korps to form a new defensive line. In the Gavray area, Krag's unit destroyed nine enemy tanks as well as a number of armored and unarmored vehicles that caused the enemy severe losses." [44]

Following this engagement, Krag's men fought with success along with his former Sturmgeschützabteilung and Regiment "Deutschland" in the Mortain area. Then these two units were ordered by the Division to partially withdraw. These were the opening movements of the Falaise battles during which the allies trapped large numbers of the retreating German forces in August 1944.

During the July 1944 Coutance battles, Krag was wounded on July 26th for which he was awarded the Wound Badge in Gold. In early August he was again decorated with two combat awards: the Tank Assault Badge 2nd grade on August 2nd and the Close Combat Clasp in Silver on the 12th. These awards were the result of accumulating the required number of combat engagements as both commander of the Sturmgeschützabteilung and Aufklärungsabteilung.[45]

While Krag and the others were fighting near Mortain, the allies tried to circle them by taking the area south and southeast of the town. They hoped to capture Trun, which was defended by Krag's unit, II./"Der Führer" and the Sturmgeschützabteilung. Large numbers of German troops were already retreating from the developing pocket as the men of Krag's command moved to engage the enemy northeast of the town.

Facing the 1st Polish Division, Krag's Aufklärungsabteilung, with portions of the Sturmgeschützabteilung, destroyed six British tanks despite a lack of available artillery support and managed to deter their attacks. During their preparation to withdraw from the pocket, Krag received an order from II.SS-Panzer-Korps to hold his positions even if he and his men were themselves unable to escape. This explicit order was required to allow as many troops as possible to retreat in an orderly manner. This order arrived by messenger as there would be no other contact with the II.SS-Panzer-Korps or the rest of "Das Reich" for some time due to the combat situation.

At the moment his command was about to be completely surrounded, Krag ordered his remain-

44 "Vorschlag Nr.7 für die Verleihung des Ritterkreuzes des Eisernen Kreuzes," dated September 15, 1944 and signed by Otto Baum.

45 The required number of combats are listed in Krag's Soldbuch and entries are made until late January, 1945.

ing troops to breakout. Krag himself took command of the infantry that covered the remaining armored vehicles during the breakout. They managed to force a breach in the encirclement moves of the enemy toward Chambois. At this time of total confusion and near panic among the other retreating troops, Paul Hausser found his way to the command post of the Aufklärungsabteilung. Although wounded, Hausser was advised of the situation by Krag and then made his way toward the nearest Corps headquarters to assist in the evacuation of the men still leaving the pocket.[46]

Holding their positions in Chambois, Krag and his men allowed large numbers of troops to escape the allied offensive. The commander of the "Leibstandarte," SS-Brigadeführer "Teddy" Wisch, was rescued by men of Krag's command after being wounded in both lungs. During the retreat, a Panther unit of the Army attached itself to Krag's command and following his instructions they assisted in the defense. Facing a sea of allied armor and infantry units the commander of "Das Reich," Otto Baum, ordered Krag to pull back toward Rouen in an effort to cross the Seine River and reach the safety of a restructured front line. Krag's men faced continuous enemy pressure and fought through the town of Elboeuf along side portions of Regiment "Der Führer" commanded by SS-Sturmbannführer Otto Weidinger.[47]

The bridge area at Rouen was held by SS-Obersturmbannführer Günther Wisliceny, the commander of Regiment "Deutschland." Before crossing, the reconnaissance detachment and the remainder of the assault gun detachment held a defensive area south of the bridge and allowed the other units of the Division to cross. Due to the constant allied air attacks, Krag had to cross with his men at night and safely did so with only minor losses. Thanks to the efforts of II./"Der Führer," the Sturmgeschützabteilung and Krag's Aufklärungsabteilung, a large number of troops escaped for later battles. For these units to successfully face superior allied forces with success, despite the near panic of the troops retreating past them, is a concrete example of combat discipline and bravery against overwhelming odds. Although most readers of Waffen-SS history stress the offensive successes of these units, it was their strength in defensive operations that saved numerous critical situations within the final two years of the war.

Krag led his men toward the Belgian border, but the Aufklärungsabteilung simply ran out of fuel in the town of Wassigny, and its position overrun by advanced armor units. In most similar situations, the troops would be considered captured and left for second line units to take care of. Instead of accepting this situation, Krag sent scouts to scavenge for fuel and, finally locating enough petrol for a 120-mile drive, towed this material to the detachment's empty vehicles. Refilling his vehicles, Krag moved his men away from their positions behind enemy lines and made contact with the rest of "Das Reich" for the fighting retreat toward the West Wall, losing only two semi-tracked vehicles, and began fighting again near Oisy.[48] On September 15, 1944, Otto Baum requested that Krag be awarded the Knight's Cross and on October 23rd the award was approved. In November

46 "Bericht über Kessel Falaise/Einsatz AA bei Trun," by Ernst August Krag, May 29, 1954.

47 Weidinger was awarded the Oakleaves to the Knight's Cross for these combats. See "Otto Weidinger, Knight's Cross with Oakleaves and Swords" by Mark C. Yerger, page 61.

48 "Kämpfe bei Wassigny," by Ernst August Krag, May 29, 1954.

divisional commander SS-Brigadeführer Heinz Lammerding presented the decoration to Krag in front of the assembled Aufklärungsabteilung during a ceremony in Borgentreich.[49]

By the time Krag's unit was relieved from its position on the West Wall to refit with the rest of the Division near Mayen, they had a total strength of slightly over 100 men. Following a fast resupply and rebuild, the reconnaissance detachment would be in action again during the Battle of the Bulge beginning in mid- December. For his actions as commander of the Aufklärungsabteilung in this last German offensive in the west, Krag would become the most decorated commander of the Aufklärungsabteilung.[50]

Although lacking in available fuel, Krag's Abteilung had been rebuilt to considerable strength for the offensive. With his four combat companies were semi-tracked and wheeled vehicles, both for infantry as well as others equipped with 2 cm and 7.5 cm cannons. His 4th Company also contained a mortar platoon, an engineer platoon, and an anti-tank unit. Krag would have a Kampfgruppe (battle group) under his command for the opening phase of the offensive, consisting of his Aufklärungsabteilung, 2./Sturmgeschützabteilung, I./Artillerie Regiment, 1./Pionier Bataillon, and a medical support platoon.[51]

Their initial orders were to carry out tactical reconnaissance in the Joubival area. Less than two miles from the objective, the lead units were in the town of Ottre when intense artillery fire commenced. With Krag's headquarters in the town, they were subjected to continuous heavy artillery fire for several hours until the town was completely set on fire. Due to the resulting losses, the attack on Joubival could not be undertaken. Krag's men defended Ottre from being captured and continued fighting allied airborne units, managing to capture one of their reconnaissance detachments during the start of the third week of December 1944. The fighting allowed the capture, by Krag's command, of many surprised allied units. The town of Salmchateau was taken next with supportive help from the artillery regiment led by SS-Standartenführer Karl Kreutz. With the weather now in the Division's favor, Krag was ordered to again attack toward Joubival and succeeded on Christmas Eve 1944. On Christmas Day SS-Sturmbannführer Otto Weidinger's Regiment "Der Führer" captured the small town of Malempre. The following week of combat would contain an engagement that resulted in the award of the Oakleaves to the Knight's Cross for Ernst August Krag.

"On January 2, 1945, Krag, with his reconnaissance detachment in a blocking position at Belle Haie, succeeded in holding up the strong enemy breakthrough supported by 22 tanks east of Malempre. The enemy suffered heavy casualties. In bitter, heavy fighting he succeeded in preventing a thrust through to the crossroads Baraque de Fraiture, which was important for the further

49 Letter to the author from Herr Krag dated September 30, 1987.

50 When an officer was granted an award he was often in a different position when the decoration was approved than he was for the combats that resulted in the award. Upon approval, the award document listed the current assignment and post war texts have, to some extent, been misleading as to the assignment of individuals with regard to their decorations. Only Krag (Oakleaves) and Otto Weidinger (Knight's Cross) obtained Germany's highest decoration for combat with the Aufklärungsabteilung. As an example, in the case of Weidinger his award document lists his assignment as Battle Group Commander (as he was at the time of approval) even though the award was for bravery in the field as commander of the Aufklärungsabteilung.

51 "Einsatz der 2.SS-Panzer-Division 'Das Reich' Aufklärungsabteilung während der Ardennenoffensive 1944/45" by Ernst August Krag, May 29, 1954.

conduct of the battle. In spite of open flanks on both sides, Krag withstood another heavy thrust by the enemy on January 4, 1945, causing heavy casualties for the enemy, and in a daringly led counter-attack with eight engineers, he cleared a break-in by the enemy so that by evening, our own blocking position was once again securely in our hands.

"Because Krag, despite the threat of encirclement, held his positions in front of the crossroads Baraque de Fraiture with only a small number of men and weapons, he made it possible for our other units on the right and left to withdraw, allowed the higher command to make changes of position which had become urgently necessary, forced the enemy to regroup, and frustrated the enemy breakthrough to the southeast."[52]

Divisional Commander Heinz Lammerding filed the above report on January 11, 1945, and after being approved by SS Army Commander SS-Oberst-Gruppenführer Sepp Dietrich, the award was approved on February 28, 1945. Ernst August Krag became the 755th soldier of the German Armed Forces awarded the Oakleaves to the Knight's Cross. It was the only Oakleaves awarded for actions by a member of the "Das Reich" reconnaissance detachment.

Losses were heavy during the last battles in the west, and "Das Reich" with the other major units was quickly rebuilt for operations in the east. Leaving Koblenz, the Division arrived in Hungary during mid-February, 1945 with Krag's men stationed in the area of Mihalyi. Their new divisional commander was SS-Gruppenführer Werner Ostendorff and, after arriving in Hungary, Ostendorff presented Ernst August Krag his Oakleaves at "Das Reich" headquarters.[53]

The final weeks of combat in the east must have had a degree of intensity beyond comprehension. Most replacements were poorly trained and under-equipped. That the units survived at all was due to the few remaining original cadre. Krag's men were placed on the line between I. and II.SS-Panzer-Korps near Kaloz, east of Lake Balaton.

In March the enormous Soviet offensive began, and the understrength units of Sepp Dietrich's 6.SS-Panzer-Armee, vastly outnumbered, were pushed west as the Russians attacked toward Austria. Attempting to carry out unrealistic orders, the men of Krag's command and the others of these SS units fought to the bitter end. That any survived seems a miracle due to the number of divisions they faced combined with their total lack of material support. As related in the divisional history, simple survival became a priority, and when the end of the war came, all units attempted to surrender to units of the Western powers if possible. On May 8, 1945, the day of the surrender, Krag commanded that all weapons and equipment be destroyed. He ordered the men of his Abteilung to fight through the Russian occupied and Czech controlled areas in small groups to reach British and American troops. This adventurous plan was mostly successful. Afterwards began the long and sorrowful period in British and American prisoner of war camps.

As with many Waffen-SS veterans, Krag suffered a period of imprisonment and did not return home until January 30, 1948. As with all Waffen-SS veterans, he did not obtain the pension benefits accorded the Army, Navy, and Air Force veterans. The idea that a man such as Krag, who fought on

[52] "Vorschlag für die Verleihung des Eichenlaubes zum Ritterkreuz des Eisernen Kreuzes," dated January 11, 1945 and signed by Lammerding and Dietrich.

[53] Letter to the author from Herr Krag dated September 30, 1987.

the front lines for five and a half years and was wounded six times, is not a soldier in the minds of the post-war legal bureaucracy is illogical and does not agree with the facts. This type of collective judgment is not the way a democracy is designed to operate.

Unable to find a fair career opportunity in post-war Germany, Krag became an engineer and served in this capacity with the Hilton Hotel Corporation in Istanbul. After the hotel was completed he returned to his home in Germany and worked there in construction management until his retirement.

Ernst August Krag was among the oldest members of the Association of Knight's Cross holders and remained active in this as well as his former division's association. In 1988 he authored a text and pictorial history of the reconnaissance troops of the Waffen-SS: "An der Spitze" (At the Lead). Having served his country honorably and having suffering through five years of combat, he lived in retirement with his wife Luise until his death in 1994. Besides his wife he is survived by two children and four grandchildren.

EPILOGUE

The American historian Mark C. Yerger requested that he be allowed to write a biographical account of my military career. I wish to emphasize that I agreed to Mr. Yerger's request only after I was sufficiently convinced that it was the historian's sole wish to write an objective and unbiased account. Only official documents stored in archives, authenticated notes, reports and photographs are used as references.

We were only able to accomplish the operations described in this biography because of the highest degree of courage and solidarity of all the participating comrades and because of our belief that we would succeed. In revealing the facts of the operations described I was motivated by the deeply felt desire for the truth to be told.

It is sorrowful and most regrettable that so many of our comrades, most in the flower of their youth, had to lose their lives in these operations. We survivors will never forget our loyal fellow soldiers who gave their lives for us in our defense.

The sacrifice of their lives is both a lasting testament and an obligation. That these men, who died for their country, are still denied any official respect or veneration is not only disgraceful but also an insult to their memory. Surely there can be no morally acceptable reason for this continuing disgraceful behavior.

Ernst August Krag
Niedernhausen
Summer 1994

At the Luftwaffe Fallschirmjäger (airforce paratrooper) school in Stendal, Krag (seated at left) poses with other trainees. Standing in the rear is their Luftwaffe training NCO. All are wearing Luftwaffe training smocks with Luftwaffe insignia.
In der Luftwaffenfallschirmspringerschule in Stendal. Krag (links sitzend) mit anderen Auszubildenden. Im Hintergrund stehend ist ihr Luftwaffen-Unterführer. Alle tragen die Luftwaffen-Ausbildungsuniform mit Luftwaffen-Abzeichen.

A 10.5cm battery of the artillery regiment. Under cover are infantry weapons in case of enemy infiltration to the otherwise exposed positions.
Eine 10.5cm Batterie des Artillerie-Rgts. Unter der Abdeckung befinden sich Infanteriewaffen für den Fall, daß feindliche Infanterie auf die sonst offene Stellung durchsickert.

Krag (5th from right) with other cadets are seated around one of their instructors, SS-Obersturmbannführer Dr. Rudolf Pfannenstiel.
Krag (5. von re.) mit anderen Offizieranwärtern und ihrem Ausbilder, SS-Obersturmbannführer Dr. Rudolf Pfannenstiel.

Krag (right) stands behind 1st Detachment Commander Herbert Otto Gille. At this time (summer 1940) Krag was adjutant of 1st Detachment. About to exit the car is divisional commander Paul Hausser (the vehicle is marked for divisional staff).
Krag (rechts) steht hinter I.Abteilungskommandeur Herbert Otto Gille. Zu dieser Zeit (Sommer 1940) war Krag I.Abteilungsadjutant. Hier bei der Abfahrt des Wagens des Divisionskommandeurs Paul Hausser (der Wagen trägt das Abzeichen des Div. Stabs).

Motorcycle messenger Hubert Hornik confers with Krag during the 1940 French campaign.
Kradmelder Hubert Hornik wird von Krag während des Frankreich-Feldzuges 1940 eingewiesen.

Two views of Krag with artillery regiment NCO candidates. Above: Krag, SS-Untersturmführer Walter Behrens and SS-Hauptscharführer Schulze lead a march while below Krag and SS-Stabsscharführer Deg are riding at the head of the column.
Zwei Photos von Krag mit Unterführer-Anwärtern des Art.Rgts. Oben: Krag, SS-Untersturmführer Walter Behrens und SS-Hauptscharführer Schulze führen eine Kolonne an, während Krag (unten) und SS-Stabsscharführer Deg an der Spitze der Kolonne reiten.

Krag's NCO class being reviewed with Krag in dress uniform and presenting arms with the dress sword given to him when commissioned.
Krag's Unterführer-Klasse wird gemustert mit Krag in Paradeuniform und Degen, den er mit dem Offizierspatent erhielt.

Im Namen des Führers und Obersten Befehlshabers der Wehrmacht

verleihe ich

dem

SS-Obersturmführer

K r a g, Ernst

~~Rgt.-Stabsbatterie/SS-A.R.~~

das II./SS-[illegible].R. 2

Eiserne Kreuz 1. Klasse

Im Felde, den 3. 8. 1941

(Dienstsiegel)

SS-Obergruppenführer und General
der Waffen - SS

(Dienstgrad und Dienststellung)

Krag's Iron Cross I Class document signed by Paul Hausser. Dated August 3, 1941, the document was originally for the Stabsbatterie (staff battery) but was corrected to show Krag's then current assignment.

Dokument für die Verleihung des EK I an Krag, unterzeichnet von Paul Hausser. Datiert am 3.8.1941 war es für die Stabsbatterie gedacht, wurde aber korrigiert mit der derzeitigen Zugehörigkeit Krags.

In these two photos Krag is shown with the newly accepted Sdkfz 141 assault guns in January 1943. These vehicles lack the side skirt armor seen in photos which was added after Kharkov.

Auf diesen zwei Fotos sieht man Krag mit den neuen Sdkfz 141 Sturmgeschützen in Januar 1943. Diese Fahrzeuge haben noch nicht die Panzer-Schürzen, die man auf späteren Fotos sehen kann. Sie wurden erst an der Front nach Charkow angebracht.

Krag congratulating newly promoted enlisted men of the assault gun detachment in the winter of 1942/43.
Krag gratuliert im Winter 1942/43 den neu beförderten Rekruten der Sturmgeschützabteilung.

SS-Obersturmführer Krag as 2nd battery commander in Russia during the early months of 1943.
SS-Obersturmführer Krag als Führer der 2.Batterie Anfang 1943 in Russland.

Weapons of the assault gun detachment in late autumn 1943. With open hatches and fully elevated guns these were being used as mobile artillery.
Waffen der Sturmgeschützabteilung im späten Frühjar 1943. Mit offenen Luken und Richtgeräten werden diese als bewegliche Artillerie verwendt.

Kharkov in 1943 was among the most bitter street fighting of the war. Here SS-Obersturmführer Hartmut Braun and SS-Untersturmführer Wolfgang Otto converse along side the weapons of the assault gun detachment's 2nd battery. Krag's own vehicle "Götz von Berlichingen" is the first in line.
Charkow erlebte die erbittertsten Strassen-kämpfe des Krieges. Hier sieht man SS-Obersturmführer Hartmut Braun und SS-Untersturmführer Wolfgang Otto neben Waffen der 2./Sturmgeschützabteilung beim Diskutieren. Krag's Fahrzeug "Götz von Berlichingen" ist an der Spitze.

From the same time and location as the previous photo, this view shows Krag's 2nd battery with the muzzles of their vehicles covered for transport.
Gleiche Zeit und Ort wie auf dem vorhergehenden Bild; dies zeigt Krag's 2.Batterie mit den verdeckten Rohrmündungen ihrer Fahrzeuge für den Transport.

Krag and his command vehicle "Götz von Berlichingen."
Krag und seine Befehlswagen "Götz von Berlichingen".

SS-Hauptsturmführer Ernst August Krag

BESITZZEUGNIS

DEM

SS-Hauptsturmführer Ernst K r a g

(NAME, DIENSTGRAD)

2./SS-Sturmgeschütz-Abt. "Das Reich"

(TRUPPENTEIL, DIENSTSTELLE)

IST AUF GRUND

SEINER AM 3. August 1943 ERLITTENEN

3 MALIGEN VERWUNDUNG – BESCHÄDIGUNG

DAS

VERWUNDETENABZEICHEN

IN S i l b e r

VERLIEHEN WORDEN.

Jm Felde, DEN 4. Aug. 1943

Kniep

(UNTERSCHRIFT)

SS-Sturmbannführer und Abteilungs-Kommandeur

(DIENSTGRAD UND DIENSTSTELLE)

Document for Krag's Wound Badge in Silver listing his 3rd wound (August 3, 1943) after his vehicle hit a mine. The document was issued the follwing day and is signed by assault gun detachment commander Walter Kniep.

Dokument über Krags Verwundetenabzeichen in Silber bestätigt seine 3. Verwundung (3.8.1943) als sein Fahrzeug auf eine Mine fuhr. Das Dokument wurde am folgenden Tag von Abteilungskommandeur Walter Kniep unterzeichnet.

From left: Hermann Bolte (German Cross in Gold July 2, 1944), Friedrich-Wilhelm Graun (German Cross in Gold September 16, 1943), Ernst August Krag, Wolfgang Otto (German Cross in Gold March 12, 1944 with Battle Group "Das Reich") and Hartmut Braun. Bolte and Otto wear single handed tank destruction strips on their right arms. Krag's command vehicle "Götz von Berlichingen" is in the background of this late autumn 1943 photo.

Von links: Hermann Bolte (Deutsches Kreuz in Gold 2. Juli 1944), Friedrich-Wilhelm Graun (Deutsches Kreuz in Gold 16. September 1943), Ernst August Krag, Wolfgang Otto (Deutsches Kreuz in Gold 12.März 1944 mit Kampfgruppe "Das Reich") und Hartmut Braun. Bolte und Otto tragen den 1-Hand-Panzervernichtungsstreifen auf ihrem rechten Armel. Krags Befehlswagen "Götz von Berlichingen" ist im Hintergrund. Photo wurde im Spätherbst 1943 aufgenommen.

Vorläufiges Besitzzeugnis

Im Namen des Führers
und Obersten Befehlshabers
der Wehrmacht

verleihe ich

dem

SS-Obersturmführer K r a g
Bttr.Fhr.2./SS-Stu.Gesch.
Abt. 2

das

Deutsche Kreuz in Gold

HQu OKH, den 9. April 1943

Oberkommando des Heeres

Generalfeldmarschall

Krag's award document for the German Cross in Gold dated April 9, 1943 with stamped signature of Feldmarschall Keitel.

Datiert 9. April 1943, trägt Krags ursprüngliches Dokument für die Verleihung des Deutschen Kreuzes in Gold die gestempelte Unterschrift von Feldmarschall Keitel.

Wolfgang Roehder (with Knight's Cross), Krag and Walter Reininghaus (battery chief) in May 1944. They are speaking to the assembled men of the assault gun detachment "Das Reich."
Wolfgang Roehder (mit Ritterkreuz), Krag und Walter Reininghaus (Batterie Chef) im Mai 1944. Sie sprechen zu den versammelten Männern der Sturmgeschützabteilung "Das Reich".

Krag (right) with his gun commanders in Russia during 1943. In the middle is Hartmut Braun and with back to camera is Otto Enderle.
Krag (rechts) weist seine Geschützführer ein (Russland 1943), in der Mitte Hartmut Braun, und mit dem Rücken zur Kamera ist Otto Enderle.

Krag being awarded his German Cross in Gold by "Das Reich" division commander Walter Krüger. On the right is SS-Unterscharführer Alfred Idel.
Krag wird durch den Kommandeur der Division "Das Reich", Walter Krüger, mit dem Deutschen Kreuz in Gold ausgezeichnet. Rechts steht SS-Unterscharführer Alfred Idel.

A wounded and exausted Ernst August Krag with his driver (who was later killed) in Russia during the spring of 1943.
Ein verwundeter und müder Ernst August Krag mit seinem Fahrer (später gefallen) in Russland im Frühjahr 1943.

From left to right are August Hoffmann, Krag and Otto Enderle in the summer of 1943. They wear the special assault gun uniform issued to assault gun crews.
Von links nach rechts: August Hoffmann, Krag und Otto Enderle im Sommer 1943. Auf diesem Photo tragen sie die Sturmgeschütz-Uniform, die an die Sturmgeschütz-Einheiten ausgegeben wurde.

1944: Krag in Borgentreich after his award of the Knight's Cross by SS-Brigadeführer Heinz Lammerding. In the background are armored cars of 4./ Aufklärungsabteilung.
1944: Krag in Borgentreich nach der Verleihung des Ritterkreuzes durch SS-Brigadeführer Heinz Lammerding. Im Hintergrund Panzerspähwagen der 4./Aufklärungsabteilung.

A line of armored cars of the reconnaissance detachment. The unit was created in June 1939 from SS Motorcycle Battalion II and at first contained two motorcycle companies, an armored car platoon, an anti-tank platoon and a signals platoon. It obtained its 3rd motorcycle company in April 1940. This later became part of the division Motorcycle Battalion and was rebuilt. Also, in April 1940, 4th company with heavy elements was added. When I./"Langemarck" was dissolved (1943) most of its men went to the reconnaissance detachment. 5th company was a support unit.
Eine Reihe Panzerspähwagen der Aufklärungsabteilung. Die Einheit wurde im Juni 1939 vom SS-Kradschützen Bataillon II aufgestellt und hatte anfangs 2 Kradschützenkompanien, einen Pz.-Spähzug, einen Pz.-Abwehrzug und einen Nachrichtenzug. Sie erhielt die 3.Kradschützenkompanie im April 1940; diese wurde später Teil des Div. Kradschützen Bataillon und neu aufgestellt. Im April 1940 kam ebenfalls die 4.(s)Kompanie mit schweren Teilen zur Abteilung. Als I./"Langemarck" aufgelöst wurde (1943), gingen die meisten der Männer zur Aufklärungsabteilung. Die 5.Kompanie war eine Begleitkompanie.

A portrait of the new holder of the Knight's Cross (1944).
Portrait des neuen Ritterkreuzträgers (1944).

Krag (middle) with Köhler (right) after being wounded by a mine (Russia 1943). On the left is Dr. Georg Christian who in 1944 became detachment medical officer.
Krag (Mitte) mit Köhler (rechts) nach Verwundung durch eine Landmine (Russland 1943). Links ist Dr. Georg Christian, der 1944 Abteilungsarzt wurde.

The Commander in assault gun uniform after his promotion to SS-Sturmbannführer on April 20, 1944.
Der Kommandeur in Sturmgeschütz-Uniform nach seiner am 20. April 1944 erfolgten Beförderung zum SS-Sturmbannführer.

Krag (right) with August Hoffmann and Otto Enderle observe an enemy air attack in Russia during the summer of 1943. They wear camouflage uniforms as compared to the field uniform seen in the previous photo.
Krag mit August Hoffmann und Otto Enderle beobachten einen feindlichen Luftangriff in Russland im Sommer 1943. Beachte die Tarnanzüge im Vergleich zur Felduniform, die auf dem vorhergehenden Bild getragen wird.

Shown during sightseeing in France after the invasion are: Krag (middle) and (left) Knight's Cross holder SS-Sturmbannführer Helmut Schreiber of Regiment "Deutschland." Schreiber won the German Cross in Gold on April 9, 1943 in command of 10./"Deutschland" and the Knight's Cross on July 30, 1943. On the right is Dr. Georg Christian.

Besichtigung der Sehenswürdigkeiten in Frankreich vor der Invasion: Krag (Mitte) und (links) Ritterkreuzträger SS-Sturmbannführer Helmut Schreiber vom Regiment "Deutschland". Schreiber erhielt das Deutsche Kreuz in Gold am 9. April 1943 als Chef der 10./"Deutschland" und sein Ritterkreuz am 30. Juli 1943. Rechts ist Dr. Georg Christian.

SS-Sturmbannführer Ernst August Krag, the 755th soldier of the German Armed Forces awarded the Oakleaves to the Knight's Cross and last armored reconnaissance detachment commander of the 2.SS-Panzer-Division "Das Reich."
SS-Sturmbannführer Ernst August Krag, 755. Soldat der Wehrmacht, dem das Ritterkreuz mit Eichenlaub verliehen wurde, und letzter Kommandeur der Panzer-Aufklärungsabteilung, 2.SS-Panzer-Division "Das Reich".

SS-Sturmbannführer
ERNST AUGUST KRAG

Träger des
Ritterkreuzes mit Eichenlaub

Kommandeur
SS-Sturmgeschützabteilung 2
SS-Panzer-Aufklärungsabteilung 2

"Das Reich"

by

Mark C. Yerger

Frau Luise Krag
gewidmet

ANMERKUNGEN

Meinen Dank die folgenden Personen für ihren Rat und Hilfe:
Otto Baum
Leslie DiNizo
Jen Hayes
Ernst August Krag
Karl Kreutz
Fritz Langanke
Jess T. Lukens
John P. Moore
Phil A. Nix
Ruth Sommers
Frank Weaver
Otto Weidinger

Truppenkameradschaft "DF"

VORWORT

Es ist besonders dankenswert, daß der amerikanische Historiker Mark C. Yerger, mit dem ich seit Jahren in einem regen Kontakt stehe, es sich zur Aufgabe gemacht hat, Biografien von ehemaligen Angehörigen der Waffen-SS zu machen.

Seiner Bitte, zu der vorliegenden Biografie von Ernst August Krag ein Vorwort zu schreiben, komme ich besonders gerne nach, kenne ich doch Ernst August Krag schon seit dem Anfang seiner Militärlaufbahn in der 5.Kompanie "Germania" in Arolsen 1936. In dieser Zeit war ich SS-Untersturmführer und Zugführer in der gleichen Einheit. Gemeinsam wurden wir 1938 mit der Ausbildungskader "Der Führer" nach Klagenfurt in Österreich versetzt. Dort trennten sich unsere Wege, weil ich erneut versetzt wurde. Wir trafen uns erst wieder im Sommer 1944 in Frankreich. Er war inzwischen Kommandeur der Aufklärungsabteilung "Das Reich" und ich führte diese Division in Personalunion mit der Division "Götz von Berlichingen" bis ich im Oktober 1944 zu einer anderen Verwendung versetzt wurde.

Mit Ernst August Krag würdigt der Verfasser zu Recht einen Soldaten der ehemaligen Waffen-SS wie es in dieser Elitetruppe in allen Dienstgraden viele gegeben hat. Sie waren nicht nur Befehlende, sie waren Führer ihrer Soldaten in allen Lagen und stets bereit, ohne Rücksicht auf das eigene Leben, alles auch zu tun, was sie von ihren Soldaten verlangten.

Diese Einsatzbereitschaft befähigte die Truppe zu den enormen Leistungen, die ihr an allen Fronten dieses gewaltigen Krieges abverlangt wurden und die heute von allen ehemaligen Gegnern respektvoll anerkannt werden. Es war der Glaube an das Vaterland, der diese Männer beseelte.

Otto Baum
Hechingen-Stetten
1995

EINFÜHRUNG

Dies ist meine 4. Biographie fur einen Ritterkreuzträger der Waffen-SS und - wie bei meinen vorhergehenden Arbeiten - bin ich bestrebt, offizielle Unterlagen in Kombination mit persönlichen Erinnerungen aufzuzeichnen. Die Berufsoffiziere der Waffen-SS kamen aus allen Schichten der Bevölkerung und leiteten eine neue Periode der militärischen Entwicklung ein, die es jedem erlaubte, allein auf der Basis seiner Leistung aufzusteigen im Vergleich zu der alten, klassifizierteren Struktur der Streitkräfte, die ebenfalls während der gleichen Periode bestand. Ernst August Krag gehörte zu der Gruppe, deren komplette Vorkriegsausbildung unter Paul Hausser ihm zugute kam, und er sollte einer der höchst-dekorierten und respektierten Kommandeure der Aufklärungsabteilung werden. Hier möchte ich meinen persönlichen Eindruck vorbringen, der auf mehreren Jahren Korrespondenz und persönlichem Kennenlernen basiert. Er war nur an den Aufzeichnungen seiner früheren Soldatenzeit interessiert und sehr bescheiden hinsichtlich seines eigenen Platzes in der Geschichte. Sein Beitrag zu historischen Untersuchungen und seine eigenen Aufzeichnungen bestätigen die obige Aussage und zahlreiche Kameraden haben mir auch das Letztere bestätigt. Sein Mut auf dem Schlachtfeld wird durch seine Auszeichnung des Eichenlaubs zum Ritterkreuz und des Verwundetenabzeichens in Gold bestätigt. Seine Tapferkeit im Kampf wird auch durch seinen Platz innerhalb der offiziellen Geschichte der 2.SS-Panzer-Division "Das Reich" bewiesen. Der Respekt, den er unter seinen Kameraden genießt, ist bis heute geblieben, ein halbes Jahrhundert nach den Ereignissen des 2. Weltkrieges.

Mark C. Yerger
1996

ERNST AUGUST KRAG

Geboren in Wiesbaden-Erbenheim am 20.2.1915, meldete sich Ernst August Krag im Mai 1935 freiwillig zum Dienst in der SS-Verfügungstruppe. Er wurde der 5./"Germania" zur Grundausbildung zugeteilt und 7 Monate später zum SS-Sturmmann befördert. Krag sollte seine gesamte Dienstzeit in der späteren Division "Das Reich" oder in einer ihr vorangegangenen Unterabteilung verbringen.

Nach 2 Jahren in "Germania" meldete sich Krag im Mai 1937 freiwillig zur Fallschirmspringerausbildung in der Luftwaffenfallschirmspringerschule in Stendal. Er besuchte den Lehrgang zusammen mit Rekruten des 3./Regiment "Hermann Göring". Dieser dauerte bis 25. Juli 1937 und Krag beendete seine Ausbildung mit 6 Absprüngen, die ihn dazu qualifizierten, das Luftwaffen-Fallschirmspringer-Abzeichen zu tragen. Nach dieser Ausbildung kehrte Krag für die verbleibenden Monate des Jahres 1937 zur 5./"Germania" zurück.

Als im Frühjahr 1938 das 3.Regiment der SS-Verfügungstruppe unter SS-Standartenführer Georg Keppler aufgestellt wurde, wechselte Krag zu der neuen SS-Standarte 3 (später "Der Führer") und wurde zu der in Klagenfurt stationierten 9.Kompanie versetzt, einer Abteilung des III.Bataillons unter SS-Sturmbannführer Hilmar Wäckerle. Krag gehörte zu dem ausgebildeten Kader dieser Einheit, die hauptsächlich aus österreichischen Rekruten bestand. In diesem neuen Aufgabengebiet wurde Krag am 1.7.1938 zum SS-Unterscharführer befördert.

Das Militärschulsystem, das qualifizierte Offiziers-Anwärter für die SS-Verfügungstruppe ausbilden sollte, war voll errichtet als Krag für einen Führerlehrgang am 1. November 1938 ausgewählt wurde und die Schule in Bad Tölz besuchte. Dies war der letzte Vorkriegslehrgang unter Leitung von SS-Standartenführer Werner Freiherr von Schele und dauerte bis zum 22. August 1939.[1] Nach 7 Monaten Ausbildung erfolgte am 15. Januar 1939 Krag's Beförderung zum SS-Junker. Am 1. Juni 1939 wurde er zum SS-Standartenjunker befördert und am 1.September 1939 zum Standartenoberjunker. Die Verleihung von Offizierspatenten erfolgte immer an traditionellen Daten, und so wurde Krag am 9. November 1939 zum SS-Untersturmführer befördert.

Verschiedene Spezialeinheiten der SS-Verfügungstruppe in einen Grosskampfverband zusammenzufassen, war eine Möglichkeit, die bereits bei der Aufstellung der ersten Einheiten im Jahre 1935 in Betracht gezogen wurde. Die letzte Einheit, die geschaffen und zuerst der Division zugeteilt werden sollte, aus der "Das Reich" später hervorging, war die Artillerie. Dieses Regiment wurde Anfang Juni 1939 in der Heeres-Artillerieschule in Jüterbog aufgestellt und von SS-Obersturmbannführer Peter Hansen[2] befehligt. Krag und andere Junker aus Bad Tölz und Braunschweig wurden diesem Regiment zugeteilt und absolvierten den ersten Artillerie-Offiziers-Bewerber-Lehrgang vom 23.8. bis 17.10.1939.

Jede Abteilung des Regiments hatte drei Batterien und eine leichte Artilleriekolonne. Jede Batterie hatte einen Beobachtungsoffizier und einen Batterieoffizier, die einem Batteriechef unterstanden. Krag wurde SS-Obersturmbannführer Herbert Gille's I.Abteilung als Batterieoffizier der 3. Batterie zugeteilt, nachdem er den Offiziersanwärterlehrgang absolviert hatte.[3] Mitte Oktober 1939 wurde das Regiment nach Pilsen verlegt und in die neue SS-V.T.-Division (mot.) unter Führung von Paul Hausser eingegliedert. Hausser hatte die SS-Junkerschule Braunschweig gegründet und war der dienstälteste SS-Offizier, der sich massgeblich an der Entwicklung der Waffen-SS beteiligte. Dieser für Krag - was seine Karriere betraf - einmalige und einflussreichste Offizier führte die Division bis zu seiner Verwundung im Oktober 1941.[4]

Während die Division in der Aufstellung begriffen war und sich mit dem Einsatz einer einzigen Kampfgruppe befasste, lief Krag's spezialisierte Ausbildung weiter. Mit anderen jungen Offizieren des Artillerie-Rgts. durchlief er einen Nachrichten-Lehrgang an der Heeres-Nachrichtenschule in Halle, der von Anfang Januar 1940 bis ll.2.1940 dauerte. Nach Rückkehr zu seiner Einheit wurde Krag Abteilungsadjutant. Diese Stellung behielt er während des gesamten Westfeldzuges der Division inne. Am 25.7.1940 wurde ihm das Eiserne Kreuz 2.Klasse verliehen. Nach dem Westfeldzug wurde die Division in Holland zum Küstenschutz eingesetzt und führte ihren eigenen Ausbildungsplan dabei weiter fort.

---

1 Schele war Lehrer an der Junkerschule Braunschweig ehe er nach Bad Tölz versetzt wurde. 1942 wurde er als SS-Oberführer pensioniert, nachdem er zum Stab des SS-Oberabschnitt "Süd" gehört hatte und seinen letzten Dienstgrad am 15.2.1940 erreichte.

2 Da man keinen erfahrenen Artillerie-Kommandeur hatte, wurde am 1. Juni 1939 Hansen vom Heer zur SS/VT mit dem Dienstgrad eines SS-Obersturmbannführers versetzt. Bis dahin war er Kommandeur der Artillerie-Abteilung 50 (14.Infanterie Division). Er verließ die Division im September 1941, diente in verschiedenen artillerieverwandten Stabspositionen im SS-Führungshauptamt bis Februar 1943. Bis Kriegsende war er in verschiedenen Stabs-und Kommandeurstellungen tätig, zuletzt als Chef des Stabes, XVIII.SS-Armee-Korps. Am 30.1.1942 wurde er zum SS-Brigadeführer befördert.

3 Bei der Aufstellung des Regiments wurde Gille erster Kommandeur der I.Abteilung, bis dahin hatte er das II./"Germania" geführt. Im Dez. 1940 verließ er die Division, um die Führung des Artillerie-Regiments der neuen Division "Germania" (später in "Wiking" umbenannt) zu übernehmen. Er wurde am 1. Mai 1943 Kommandeur dieser Division und am 20. Juli 1944 Kommandeur des IV.SS-Panzer-Korps. Am 28.2. 1942 wurde ihm das Deutsche Kreuz in Gold und am 8.10.1942 als Artillerie-Regimentskommandeur das Ritterkreuz verliehen. Das Eichenlaub erhielt er am 1.Nov. 1943 als Divisionskommandeur und die Schwerter am 20.2. 1944. Die Brillanten zum Ritterkreuz wurden ihm am 20. 4. 1944 verliehen. Seine letzte Beförderung zum SS-Obergruppenführer erfolgte am 9.11.1944.

4 Siehe "SS-Oberst-Gruppenführer Paul Hausser" von Mark C. Yerger zur Karriere des dienstältesten Waffen-SS Kommandeurs.

Krag blieb bis Ende 1940 offiziell Abteilungsadjutant. Ab Mitte September wurde er Zugführer in der 1.Unterführer-Lehrbatterie in Amersfoort/Holland, die Unterführer ausbildete. Krag führte diese Unterführer-Anwärter bis zur 2. Woche Dezember.

Im April 1940 wurde eine schwere Abteilung des Regiments einsatzbereit, und Krag wurde im Frühjahr 1941 wieder Batterieführer der 11.Batterie dieser Abteilung.[5] IV.(s)Abteilung war mit schweren 15 cm Fernkampf-Geschützen unter der Führung von SS-Hauptsturmführer Karl Kreutz [6] ausgerüstet. Krag behielt diese Stellung während des kurzen Jugoslawien-Feldzuges und wurde am 20.4.1941 zum SS-Obersturmführer befördert. Anschliessend bereitete sich die Division auf die bevorstehende Offensive in Sowjet-Russland vor, bei der Krag in den ersten Kampfmonaten die 5.Batterie unter dem Kommandeur der II.Abteilung, SS-Sturmbannführer Max Wunder, führte.

Das schnelle Vorrücken in den ersten Monaten bei BARBAROSSA hatte schwere Kämpfe zur Folge und stellte an die Angehörigen der Division erhöhte taktischen Anforderungen, da die Einheiten oft schneller vorrückten als dies ihre unterstützenden Waffen konnten; eine Situation, die besonders durch die physisch komplizierten Einheiten, wie z.B. das Artillerie-Regiment, wahrgenommen wurde. Am 27.7.1941 wurde Krag das Eiserne Kreuz 1.Klasse für seine Leistungen in dieser Anfangsphase des Feldzuges verliehen.

Bei den schweren Kämpfen um Jelnja entstanden in den untergeordneten Einheiten der Division schneller Verluste als Ersatz für sie herangeschafft werden konnte. Bei der Ausdehnung der Kämpfe nach Mittelrussland wurden zeitweise Stabsbatterien als vorübergehender Ersatz eingesetzt. Unterversorgt, was Winterbekleidung und andere dringend benötigten Versorgungsgüter anbelangt, kämpfte die Division als Schwerpunkteinheit bei dem Versuch, Moskau einzunehmen. Die Härte, die Krag und andere Angehörige der Division im ersten Russland-Winter ertragen mussten, kann nur von den Männern nachempfunden werden, die dabei waren. Die Verluste an jungen Offizieren waren aufgrund der Eigenschaft, ihre Truppe bei den Kämpfen immer vorn zu führen, schwer. Als "Reich" im Dezember 1941 in ihre neue Stellung südwestlich von Sytschevka wechselte, wurde Krag zur Aufklärungsabteilung unter Führung von SS-Hauptsturmführer Wilhelm Kment als Kompanie-Führer der 2. Kompanie versetzt.[7] Bei Sytschevka, wo auch Teile der 1.Panzer-Divison im Einsatz waren, wurde Krag am 23.1.1942 schwer verwundet. Stärkere russischen Infanterie-Teile waren in der Nacht zum 23.1. bei klirrender Kälte und starkem Schneetreiben teilweise durch die nur schwach besetzten Sicherungslinien der Aufklärungsabteilung vorgedrungen und standen bis kurz vor dem Abteilungs-Gefechtsstand. In einem für beide Seiten harten, verlustreichen Nahkampf gelang es, die Russen wieder zurückzuwerfen.

Krag wurde nach erster ärztlicher Versorgung nach Loetzen/Ostpr. in ein Lazarett eingeliefert und später zur endgültigen Genesung in ein Mainzer Krankenhaus verlegt. Der Großteil der stark angeschlagenen Division, ausser einer Kampfgruppe, geführt vom 1. Generalstabsoffizier der Division, Werner Ostendorff, wurde herausgelöst und zur Neuaufstellung zunächst nach Fallingbostel verlegt.

Während Krag's Wiederherstellung übernahm SS-Gruppenführer Georg Keppler die Division und damit die Führung der an Umfang grössten Einheit, die am 1.4. 1942 neu aufgestellt wurde. Nach dieser Neuaufstellung wurde mit Datum vom 9.11.1942 der Name der Division in SS-Panzer-Grenadier-Division "Das Reich" umbennant.[8] Krag kehrte am 1.3.42 zum Artillerie-Regiment zurück.[9] Aufgrund seiner organisatorischen Fähigkeiten, die er als Abteilungsadjutant und im Kampf bewiesen hatte, wurde er Regimentsadjutant des neuen Artillerie-Kommandeurs, SS-Standartenführer Kurt Brasack.[10] Dies sollte seine letzte Stellung innerhalb dieser Einheit werden, der er seit seiner Berufung zum Offizier angehörte.

---

[5] Die schwere Abteilung wurde anfangs als V.Abteilung bezeichnet, während die zuerst aufgestellte IV.Abteilung für die "Leibstandarte" unter der Führung der Division gebildet wurde. In ihrer früheren Form unter der Führung von SS-Sturmbannführer Karl Rees, wurden die schweren Batterien mit 13, 14 und 15 numeriert. Nachdem ihre Abt.-Nr. geändert wurde, erhielten die Batterien die Bezeichnung 10, 11 und 12.

[6] Kreutz führte die 2. Batterie (Juni 1939 bis Feb. 1941) und die 6. Batterie (Feb. bis Apr. 1941), ehe er die Führung der IV.Abteilung im April 1941 übernahm. Als Abteilungskommandeur wurde ihm am 17. Dez. 1943 das Deutsche Kreuz in Gold verliehen. Nachdem er das gesamte Artillerie-Regiment im März 1943 übernommen hatte, wurde ihm auch am 5.9.1944 das Ritterkreuz und am 6.3.1945 das Eichenlaub für dieses Kommando verliehen. Er führte zweimal "Das Reich", (20.1.1945 bis 4.2.1945 und 18.4.1945 bis zur Kapitulation). Am 20.4.1945 wurde er zum SS-Standartenführer befördert.

[7] Stellung bestätigt durch Eintragung im Soldbuch. Kopie genehmigt durch Herrn Krag. Zur Laufbahn von Wilhelm Kment siehe "Otto Weidinger, Ritterkreuz mit Eichenlaub und Schwertern", Fußnote 16.

[8] Die Division hatte in ihrer Geschichte sieben Bezeichnungen: 10.10.39 bis 1.4.40 SS-V.T.-Division (mot.), 1.4.40 bis 30.11.40 SS-V.-Division, 1.12.40 bis 27.1.41 SS-Division "Deutschland", 28.1.41 bis 5.42 SS-Division "Reich", 5.42 bis 9.11.42 SS-Division "Das Reich", 9.11.42 bis 1.44 SS-Panzer-Grenadier-Div. "Das Reich" und 1.44 bis Kriegsende 2. SS-Panzer-Grenadier-Division "Das Reich". Bei solchen Daten, die mit dem vorangegangenen Text nicht übereinstimmen, hat der Autor Daten aus den SS-FHA-Direktiven, von Himmler unterzeichnet, aus der National Archives Records-Group T-175 entnommen. Einige Daten wurden zu einem späteren Zeitpunkt in das Divisions-Tagebuch (KTB) eingetragen.

[9] SS-Führungshauptamt, Kommandoamt der Waffen-SS, IIa AZ: 21c 16/Br./FHu. "Personalverfügung".

[10] Brasack kam vom Kommando des I./Artillerie-Rgts. "Wiking"; er begann seine Laufbahn mit der Führung des I./Art.Rgts. "Totenkopf". Als Herbert Vahl im März 1943 verwundet wurde, übernahm Brasack die Division, nachdem er das Regiment seit Januar 1942 geführt hatte. Brasack unterzeichnete als Div. Kommandeur die Empfehlung für das Deutsche Kreuz in Gold für Krag. Nachdem er die Division verlassen hatte, war er Nachschubkommandeur der Waffen-SS und Polizei "Ostland" und beendete den Krieg als Arko (dienstältester Artillerie-Kommandeur) des IV.SS-Panzer-Korps. Am 1.1. 1945 wurde er zum Brigadeführer befördert und erhielt am 9.10.1944 das Deutsche Kreuz in Gold für die Führung des SS-Artillerie-Rgts. 54.

Als Regimentsadjutant war es Krag's Aufgabe, bei der Neuaufstellung die starken Verluste des Regiments im vorangegangenen Jahr schnellstmöglich aufzufüllen. Drei mittlere Batterien und zwei schweren Kalibers sowie mehrere Stabsbatterien wurden vollständig neu aufgestellt.[11] Zusätzlich dazu wurde die Einheit auf Selbstfahrlafetten vorbereitet, die in die I.Abteilung eingegliedert und wesentlich zur Angriffskraft des Regiments beitragen sollte. Für Nahkämpfe des vergangenen Jahres wurde Krag am 14.7.42 mit dem Infanterie-Sturmabzeichen und am 3.8.42 mit der Ostmedaille ausgezeichnet. Während dieser langwierigen Neuaufstellung erhielt die Division endlich auch Panzer.

Eine Panzer-Abteilung wurde im April 1942 aufgestellt, und gleichzeitig mit der Erweiterung dieser Einheit zu einem Panzer-Regiment kam im Oktober 1942 eine Sturmgeschützabteilung zur Division.[12] Unter der Führung des früheren Kommandeurs von III./"Deutschland", SS-Hauptsturmführer Walter Kniep, gab es folgende massgebende Offiziere in der neu-aufgestellten Einheit:

Abteilungskommandeur	SS-Hauptsturmführer Walter Kniep
Abteilungsadjutant	SS-Untersturmführer d.R. Heinrich Köhler
Abteilungsarzt	SS-Obersturmführer Dr. Fritz Sedlaczek
Verwaltungsführer:	SS-Obersturmführer Fritz Dietrich
TFK I:	SS-Obersturmführer Anton Beinl
TFK (W):	SS-Untersturmführer Fritz Brune
Stabsbatterie Chef	SS-SS-Obersturmführer Friedrich-Wilhelm Graun
1.Batterie Chef	SS-Obersturmführer Eberhard Telkamp[13]
2.Batterie Chef	SS-Obersturmführer Ernst August Krag
3.Batterie Chef	SS-Obersturmführer Siegfried Kepp[14]

Jede Batterie hatte 7 Geschütze von normaler Stärke. Eingeteilt in 3 Züge, waren Krags Zugführer: SS-Untersturmführer Steffen Chemnitz, SS-Untersturmführer August Hoffmann und SS-Untersturmführer Otto Enderle. Nachdem Krag sein neues Kommando übernommen hatte, nahm er an einem Lehrgang für Sturmgeschütze in Jüterbog mit dem Lehrstab der Schule vom 8.11 bis 15.12.42 teil. Die Abteilung erhielt ihre Sdkfz 141's ausgerüstet mit 7.5 cm Kanonen, im Debica-Ausbildungszentrum in Polen und wurde im Januar 1943 vor dem Einsatz in Russland schnell mit ihren neuen Waffen vertraut gemacht. Deutlich beeindruckt von Krag's Leistungen innerhalb von nur 3 Monaten, reichte Kommandeur Kniep ihn im Januar 1943 zur Beförderung zum SS-Hauptsturmführer ein.

Als "Das Reich" und "Leibstandarte" im Januar 1943 nach Russland zum Einsatz kamen, bildeten sie das SS-Panzer-Korps unter Führung von Paul Hausser. Im folgenden Monat - vereint mit "Totenkopf" - verbrachten alle drei Divisionen die meiste Zeit des Jahres 1943 mit ununterbrochenen Kampfeinsätzen, die bereits kurz nach ihrem Eintreffen begannen.

Am 15.2.43 führte Krag seine Batterie zusammen mit 3./Pionier Bataillon und 5./"Der Führer" bei zähen Kämpfen entlang der Strasse zwischen Kulnitschi und Terehoff und vernichtete grosse Mengen an Material. Damit erfüllte er die ihm erteilte Aufgabe. Kennzeichnende Anerkennung der Leistung seiner Untergebenen sollte später bei seinem Bericht die Grundlage für die Verleihung des Deutschen Kreuzes in Gold an einen seiner Geschützführer, SS-Unterscharführer Alfred Idel, bilden.[15]

Später im Februar musste "Das Reich" bei ihrem Vorstoss auf Pawlograd mehrere Brücken erobern. Die Kämpfe um diese drei Eisenbahnbrücken waren die Vorbedingung für den weiteren Vormarsch der Division auf die Stadt am Samara-Fluss. Dem II./"Der Führer" unter SS-Obersturmbannführer Silvester Stadler wurde befohlen, alle drei Übergänge zu besetzen.[16]

"Am 21 Februar 1943 wurde dem II./'Der Führer' befohlen, einen Brückenkopf bei Pawlograd zu bilden und zu halten und danach die drei Brücken zu überqueren. Die erste Brücke konnte durch direkten Angriff genommen werden.

---

11 SS-FHA Org.Tgb.Nr. 66/42 g.Kdos. "Gliederung der SS-Div. "Reich", datiert vom 5.März 1942.

12 SS-Führungshauptamt Kdo.Amt.d.Waffen-SS, Org. Tgb. Nr 476/42 g.Kdos. "Aufstellung von Panzer-und Sturmgeschützeinheiten für das SS-Panzer-Regiment 2, für die Sturmgeschütz-Abteilung 2 der SS-Division "Das Reich", datiert vom 14.10.42.

13 Verleihung des Deutschen Kreuzes in Gold am 28.2.42 als Sturmgeschütz-Kommandant der einzigen Batterie, die schon vorher bestanden hatte und dem Artillerie-Regiment unterstellt war. Sie wurde aufgelöst, ehe die Abteilung aufgrund von Ausfällen aufgestellt wurde. Er verliess die Division, um Panzer-Abteilungskommandeur der 9.SS-Panzer-Division "Hohenstaufen" zu werden, wo er am 23.8.44 das Rittenkreuz erhielt. Später führte er das Panzer-Regiment der Einheit und beendete den Krieg als Obersturmbannführer. In den ersten Monaten nach seiner Versetzung führte er die Sturmgeschützabteilung von "Hohenstaufen".

14 Kepp kam mit der Nachrichtenabteilung SS/VT im Jahr 1937 in die SS/VT. Nach Absolvierung der Junkerschule Braunschweig 1940 wurde er zur Division versetzt und am 9.4.43 wurde ihm das Deutsche Kreuz in Gold als Kommandeur 3./Sturmgeschütz-Abteilung verliehen. Nachdem er die Div. verlassen hatte, diente er bei verschiedenen Sturmgeschütz-Ausbildungs- und Ersatz-Einheiten sowie als Lehrer in der SS-Sturmgeschützschule Janowitz. In dieser Stellung wurde er am 1.1.45 zum Sturmbannführer ernannt.

15 "Vorschlagsliste fur die Verleihung des Deutschen Kreuzes in Gold" datiert vom 20..3.43. Idel kam zur Sturmgeschütz-Abt. von der 5./"Der Führer". Ihm wurde das Deutsche Kreuz in Gold am 15.4.43 als SS-Unterscharführer und Geschützführer verliehen.

16 Betr. Silvester Stadler's Laufbahn siehe "Otto Weidinger, Ritterkreuz mit Eichenlaub und Schwerten" von Mark C. Yerger, Fußnote 34.

Dann verstärkte sich der Feindwiderstand und es schien, als ob der Angriff zum Stillstand kommen würde, hauptsächlich deswegen, weil ein weiteres Vordringen der Sturmgeschütze aufgrund des starken Panzer-Abwehrfeuers unmöglich schien.

"Nach eigener Entscheidung griff SS-Obersturmführer Krag mit seiner Batterie über die erste Brücke an, zerstörte drei Panzer-Abwehrgeschütze und mehrere Maschinengewehrstellungen. Durch diese Aktion konnte unsere eigene Infanterie über die 2. und 3. Brücke vorankommen. Somit unterstützte Krag den Angriff und hatte einen wesentlichen Anteil am Erfolg des Bataillons, da dies eine Bedingung für den weiteren Vormarsch der Division darstellte".[17]

Zwei Tage später verlegte die Division etwas nördlich in Richtung auf Werbki für ihren nördlichen Angriff auf Losowaja, Zu dieser Zeit versuchte ein sowjetischer Gegenangriff, Pawlograd zurückzuerobern.

"Am 23. Februar 1943 verteidigte II./'Der Führer' Pawlograd im Norden. Während der Nacht brach der Feind mit 10 Panzern durch. Der Angriff wurde zurückgeschlagen, und am Morgen machte 7./'Der Führer' und 2./ Sturmgeschützabteilung unter dem Befehl von SS-Ostuf. Krag einen Gegenangriff. Unter SS-Obersturmführer Krag's erfahrener Führung bei der Unterstützung des Angriffs wurden 1 Panzer-Abwehrgeschütz und 6 Maschinengewehrstellungen zerstört. Hierdurch konnte die 7./'Der Führer' ihren Auftrag ohne eigene Verluste, aber mit 272 Verlusten auf russischer Seite, erfüllen." [18]

Nachdem Pawlograd's Verteidigungsring gesichert war, griff die Division Werbki an, den nächsten sowjetischen Stützpunkt. Die Schwere des Kampfes um die Stadt wird dadurch belegt, daß das Gefecht in Krag's Soldbuch für eine spätere Verleihung der Nahkampfspange eingetragen wurde.

"Für den Angriff auf Werbki wurde Krag's Batterie dem II./'Deutschland' unterstellt. Das erste Ziel war die Brücke nahe des südwestlichen Zugangs zur Stadt. Die grundlegende Idee war, jene Brücke in einem Überraschungsangriff zu stürmen. Krag's Batterie stieß aus diesem Grunde mit einer Gruppe Pioniere und Angehörigen der 6./'Deutschland' so schnell wie möglich nach vorn. Aber die Brücke war vermint und befand sich kurz vor der Sprengung durch die Russen. Sofort nach dem Eintreffen an der Brücke, die nun der Feind erfolgreich zerstört hatte, eröffnete SS-Obersturmführer Krag das Feuer auf die schweren Waffen des Feindes. Ihre Besatzungen verliessen fluchtartig ihre Fahrzeuge. Wir können Krag's Batterie dafür danken, daß es für unsere Infanterie möglich wurde, den südwestlichen Zugang zu Werbki sowie die südlichen Vororte ohne weitere Schwierigkeiten zu besetzen. Dieser Raum war mit Panzerabwehrwaffen sowie einigen Panzern stark befestigt worden. Unseren Kräften gelang es, diese Waffen des Feindes zu erbeuten.

"SS-Obersturmführer Krag schaltete die schweren Waffen des Feindes aus, dadurch gelang es ihm, Werbki westlich der zerstörten Brücke über den Samara zu erreichen. Er stieß sofort mit seiner Batterie weiter vom Südwesten der Stadt zum nordwestlichen Ausgang vor. Vollkommen ohne Infanteriedeckung stellten die Sturmgeschütze als erste die Verbindung mit den Angriffsspitzen der SS 'Totenkopf' Division her." [19]

Nachdem Werbki gesichert war, setzte die Division ihren Vormarsch in nordöstlicher Richtung auf Losowaja am Bratal fort. In der letzten Woche Februar 1943 wurden diese Angriffe von Krag's Batterie zur Unterstützung des Kradschützenbataillons unter Führung von SS-Sturmbannführer Jakob Fick[20] geführt. Während Krag die 3. Kompanie von Fick's Kommando unterstützte, bemerkte er einen Angriff sowjetischer Panzer auf Silvester Stadler's II./"Der Führer".

"Am 26. Februar 1943 griff das II./'Der Führer' Losowaja an. Schon während der Bereitstellung machte der Feind einen Gegenangriff, der von 3 T-34 unterstützt wurde und das II/'Der Führer' in eine kritische Lage brachte und festnagelte. Mit 2 Geschützen in der Nähe des Kradschützenbataillons beobachtete SS-Obersturmführer Krag die Lage und vernichtete zwei der Panzer. Damit rettete er die Situation. Nach Rücksprache mit dem Kommandeur des Kradschützenbatallions unterstützte Krag in aussergewöhnlicher Weise weiter die Infanterie-Angriffe des II./'Der Führer' und vernichtete 9 Panzer (T-34) und ungefähr die gleiche Anzahl Maschinengewehrstellungen." [21]

---

[17] "Begründung der Stellungnahme des Zwischenvorgesetzten" für das Deutsche Kreuz in Gold, datiert am 13. März 1943 und unterzeichnet von Kniep.

[18] ebd.

[19] ebd.

[20] Das Kradschützenbataillon wurde im Februar 1941 aufgestellt. Im Mai 1942 wurde daraus das I. Bataillon des Rgts. "Langemarck". Innerhalb der Division wurde diese Einheit jedoch immer noch "das Kradschützenbataillon" genannt. Im April 1943 wurde "Langemarck" aufgelöst und zur Verstärkung anderer Einheiten, einschl. der Aufklärungsabteilung, verwendet. Im Mai 1942 übernahm Fick den Befehl über das Bataillon, und am 23. April 1943 wurde ihm für die Führung des Bataillons das Ritterkreuz verliehen. Im April 1943 übernahm er auch die Führung der Aufklärungsabteilung, bei der er bis zu seiner Versetzung zur 17. Panzer-Grenadier-Division "Götz von Berlichingen" als Kommandeur des SS-Panzer-Grenadier-Rgts. 38 blieb. Er beendete den Krieg, nachdem er kurz diese spätere Division geführt hatte, mit dem Dienstgrad eines SS-Standartenführers. Er verließ "Das Reich" im August 1943, nachdem er seit 1934 dieser Division und der SS/VT angehört hatte.

[21] siehe Fussnote 17

Die Kämpfe setzten sich am folgenden Tag bei verstärktem sowjetischem Widerstand und Gegenangriffen fort. Um diese Zeit unterstützte Krag's Batterie wiederum die Kradschützen unter Jakob Fick's Befehl, bis Losowaja endgültig gesichert war.

"Krag's Batterie wurde am 27. Februar 1943 dem SS-Kradschützen Bataillon zugeordnet. SS-Obersturmführer Krag unterstützte den Angriff des Kradschützenbataillons im Raum nordwestlich von Losowaja sowie den nordöstlichen Teil der Stadt an der Losowaja Eisenbahnlinie. Hier trug er mit seinen mutigen Angriffen wesentlich zum Erfolg der Operation bei." [22]

Als nächstes sollte die Division im Angriff Rasdolje und bei weiterem Vorgehen Jefremowka nehmen. Für diesen Angriff wurde Krag's Batterie dem Regiment "Der Führer" unterstellt, während die 3. Batterie, die jetzt unter dem Befehl des späteren Ritterkreuzträgers Dr. Wolfgang Roehder stand, dem Regiment "Deutschland" zugeordnet wurde.

"Beim Angriff auf Rasdolje am 28. Februar 1943 erhielt die 2./Sturmgeschützabteilung zusammen mit der 5./'Der Führer' den Befehl durchzubrechen und den Ort einzunehmen. Schweres PAK-Feuer, unterstützt von mehreren Panzern, konnte den Angriff des Obersturmführers Krag nicht bremsen. Er plazierte seine Geschütze so geschickt, dass in Nahkampfgefechten 4 T-34, 3 PAK Stellungen und mehrere Maschinengewehre vernichtet werden konnten. Dies ermöglichte den Angriff und das Vorgehen der 5./'Der Führer', so dass das Ziel erreicht werden konnte." [23]

Der März 1943 begann mit Kämpfen um Jefremowka am Orel. Hier gab es im ersten Monat des Kampfes schwere Gefechte, und am Ende der ersten März- woche bestand die Sturmgeschützabteilung nur noch aus 9 Sturmgeschützen, die sie zum Kampf bereitstellen konnten.[24] Nachdem Rasdolje genommen war, galt Krag's Unterstützung weiterhin dem II./"Der Führer".

"Am 1. März 1943 stiess 'Das Reich' von Rasdolje auf Jefremowka vor. Krag fuhr mit seiner Batterie immer an der Spitze der vordersten Kompanie. Sie wollten verhindern, dass der Feind neue Verteidigungsstellungen in den Randgebieten von Jefremowka aufbauen konnte. Am nächsten Tag setzte das II./'Der Führer' seinen Angriff trotz schweren feindlichen Artillerie-, PAK-, Panzer-, Werfer-, und Maschinengewehrfeuers fort, machte aber aufgrund des Beschusses wenig Fortschritte. SS-Obersturmführer Krag näherte sich mit seiner Batterie und aufgrund seiner hervorragend gewählten Position schoss er 8 Panzer (3 T-34), 9 PAK und zahlreiche Maschinengewehrstellungen ab. Ausserdem konnten 19 Geschütze erbeutet werden, von diesen wurden wenigstens 3/4 durch Krag's Batterie während des Gefechtes vernichtet. Der Erfolg des Angriffs vom II./'Der Führer' war also hauptsächlich Krag mit seinen Sturmgeschützen zuzuschreiben."[25]

Trotz Mangel an Erfahrung mit ihren Sturmgeschützen waren Krag's Männer ein gleichwertiger Gegner gegenüber den T-34. Taktisch vorteilhafte Situationen brachten eindrucksvolle Erfolge. Mehrere der Sturmgeschützkommandanten zählten über 30 Panzerabschüsse bei den Sowjets, und man erfährt später, daß die Sturmgeschützabteilung das Jahr innerhalb der Division "Das Reich" mit einem der höchsten Prozentsätze vernichteter Fahrzeuge pro verlorener Waffe beendete. Der Kampf in der ersten Märzwoche 1943 veranlasste Walter Kniep Krag für seine Leistungen beim Vorstoß - angefangen vom Einmarsch in Russland bis zu den Kämpfen um Charkow - für das Deutsche Kreuz in Gold vorzuschlagen.

"Am 3. März 1943 war Krag's Batterie noch dem Kradschützenbataillon unterstellt. Um 6 Uhr früh griffen die Russen mit 2000 Mann in der Senke von Losowaja und auf den Höhenrücken südwestlich der Stadt an. Der Feind wurde zurückgeschlagen und durch das konzentrierte Feuer aller verfügbaren Waffen vernichtet. Dabei vernichtete Krag's Batterie eine Panzer-Abwehr-Batterie mit 4 Geschützen. Feindverluste betrugen mindestens 200 Mann, gefallen oder verwundet durch die Wirkung von Krag's Waffen.

"Am 7. und 8. März 1943 unterstützte SS-Obersturmführer Krag mit seinen Sturmgeschützen den Angriff des III./'Der Führer' auf Stanaja Vodolaga. Im Verlauf des Kampfes vernichtete Krag 2 Panzer-Abwehrgeschütze sowie 2 mit Kriegsmaterial beladene bespannte Schlitten. Feindverluste: Wenigstens 15 Gefallene und 20 Verwundete."[26]

Bei strenger Kälte und den schweren Verlusten der Division waren die heftigen Kämpfe um Charkow und Bjelgorod nicht nur ein Kampf gegen einen entschlossenen Feind, sondern auch ein Kampf gegen die Naturgewalten. Mit einigem

[22] ebd.

[23] ebd..

[24] Otto Weidinger: Division "Das Reich", Band IV, Seite 58.

[25] siehe Fussnote 17.

[26] "Vorschlagsliste Nr.1 für die Verleihung des Deutschen Kreuzes in Gold", unterzeichnet am 13..3.1943 und genehmigt durch Brasack und Hausser am 22.3.1943.

neu-angekommenen Ersatz eroberte Hausser's Korps in Nahkämpfen Charkow, obwohl - taktisch gesehen - die Vorteile auf seiten des Feindes lagen. Die Einnahme der Stadt war der größte Erfolg des Krieges für die Waffen-SS und der letzte Sieg einer Offensive gegen eine große Stadt durch die Wehrmacht.[27] Die Stadt war am 14. März 1943 fest in deutscher Hand; die Kämpfe nach Norden gegen Bjelgorod wurden in der folgenden Woche fortgesetzt. Mitte März 1943 vernichtete die Sturmgeschützabteilung zusammen mit Regiment "Deutschland" unter SS-Standartenführer Heinz Harmel 14 russische Panzer.[28]

Als Walter Kniep die Empfehlung für das Deutsche Kreuz in Gold für Krag unterzeichnete, schrieb er am Ende seines Berichtes einen Kommentar, der einen kleinen Einblick in Kniep's Urteil über Krag als Batterie-Chef gibt.

"SS-Obersturmführer Krag erwies sich als tapferer Offizier und furchtloser, schneidiger Teufelskerl bei jedem Kampfeinsatz. Er führte seine Batterie mit großem taktischen Geschick und war Vorbild an Mut und Tapferkeit für seine Unterführer und Männer." [29]

Am 9. April 1943 wurde die Auszeichnung des Deutschen Kreuzes in Gold für Krag genehmigt und ihm später durch den Divisionskommandeur, SS-Gruppenführer Walter Krüger, verliehen. Am 20. April 1943 wurde Kniep's Gesuch um Krag's Beförderung zum SS-Hauptsturmführer genehmigt und mit gleichem Datum wirksam.

Die Division erhielt eine kurze Instandsetzungspause hinter der Front, die im April 1943 begann, um sich auf die bevorstehenden Sommerkämpfe vorzubereiten, in denen die größten Panzerschlachten der Geschichte stattfinden sollten. Ersatz brachte die Sturmgeschütz-Abt. in dieser Zeit auf eine Stärke von 33 Sturmgeschützen.[30] Die Division erhielt Ersatz für ihre Panzer-Einheiten und gliederte auch in Charkow erbeutete T-34 in ihre Einheiten ein.[31]

Die vom 5. bis 17. Juli 1943 tobenden Kämpfe von extremer Härte zeigten die größten Panzer-Massierungen des Krieges; der Erfolg der Sturmgeschützabteilung wird am besten mit ihrer Anzahl Siege und anderen hierdurch bedingten Tatsachen ausgedrückt, da kein Kriegstagebuch der Abteilung aus dieser Zeit mehr existiert. Kursk stellte die besten sowjetischen Panzer-Divisionen gegen das II.SS-Panzer-Korps auf. Es gab keine in der Stärke vergleichbaren Panzer in der deutschen Wehrmacht.

Am 8. Juli 1943 wehrte die Abteilung zusammen mit Regimenter "Deutschland" und "Der Führer" einen Angriff von 170 russischen gepanzerten Fahrzeugen ab und vernichtete 92 sowjetische Panzer, von denen 51 der Abteilung gutgeschrieben wurden gegenüber nur einem eigenen Verlust.[32] In der Zeit vom 5.-17. Juli 1943 zerstörte die Sturmgeschützabteilung 129 Feindpanzer gegenüber 2 eigenen Verlusten. Walter Kniep erhielt am 14. August 1943 das Ritterkreuz in Anerkennung der Leistungen seiner Einheiten in diesen Juli-Kämpfen.[33]

Dadurch, daß Kniep Krag als seinen Nachfolger als Kommandeur der Einheit bestimmte, bescheinigt er Krag's Kampfleistung und belobigt seine Kenntnisse als Taktiker sowie seine persönliche Tapferkeit. Am 14. Juli 1943 und am 3. August 1943 wurde Krag während der Kämpfe am Mius verwundet und erhielt das Verwundetenabzeichen in Silber. Zur gleichen Zeit wurde der Abteilungsadjutant Heinrich Köhler verwundet als Krag's Befehlswagen auf eine Mine fuhr.[34] Der Wehrmachtsbericht vom 27. August 1943 beglückwünschte "Das Reich" zur Vernichtung von 1000 Feindpanzern innerhalb 35 aufgezeichneter Kampftage, angefangen mit den Kämpfen um Charkow im März. In der offiziellen Geschichtsschreibung der Division "Das Reich" werden diese Erfolge mit 500 vom Panzer-Regiment, 250 von der Sturmgeschütz-Abteilung und 250 vom Panzer-Grenadier-Regiment sowie anderen Einheiten angegeben.[35]

Eine Panzer-Abteilung von normaler Stärke umfasst 4 Kompanien mit 3 Zügen, jeder der letzteren mit 5 Fahrzeugen. Das Panzer-Regiment hatte 2 Abteilungen. Die Sturmgeschützabteilung hat 3 Batterien mit je 9 Sturmgeschützen einschliesslich des Befehlswagens. Man kann sie in der Stärke mit 2 Panzerkompanien vergleichen. Der Gesamtabschuss der alliierten Panzer durch das Panzer-Regiment und die Sturmgeschützabteilung wurde zu 50% von der

---

27 Diese Kämpfe brachten mehr Ritterkreuze und Deutsche Kreuze als irgend welche anderen Kämpfe der Waffen-SS. Siehe Krätschmer: "Die Ritterkreuzträger der Waffen-SS" und die offizielle Geschichtsschreibung der 3 hier beteiligten Divisionen.

28 Otto Weidinger, "Division Das Reich", Band IV.

29 siehe Fußnote 26.

30 II. SS-Panzer Korps, Ia Kriegstagebuch Nr. 6, Eintragung für Juli 1943.

31 Angehörige der Panzerjäger-Abt. und des Panzer-Regiments bildeten mit diesen erbeuteten. T-34 das III./Panzer-Regiment und wurden der Division unterstellt bis die Reparatur der Waffen unmöglich wurde (einige Panzer wurden fertiggestellt in einer Fabrik vorgefunden). Quellen geben 25-33 Panzer an, die in den Bestand zur Höchststärke integriert wurden. Hausser brachte 6 von ihnen nach Deutschland, um sie bei der Panzer-Abwehr-Ausbildung einzusetzen.

32 "Vorschlagsliste Nr.17 für die Verleihung des Ritterkreuzes zum Eisernen Kreuz", Antrag für das Ritterkreuz für Walter Kniep in Anerkennung der Leistungen seiner Abteilung und unterzeichnet von Walter Krüger am 31. Juli 1943. Kniep wurde das Ritterkreuz am 31. Juli 1943 verliehen nachdem er am 15. November 1941 das erste Deutsche Kreuz in Gold seiner Division erhalten hatte.

33 ebd.

34 Brief an den Autor von Herrn Krag, datiert v. 16. November 1986.

35 Otto Weidinger, "Division Das Reich", Band IV, Seite 326.

Sturmgeschützabteilung erbracht. Mit dieser Feststellung ist nicht beabsichtigt, die erbrachten Leistungen des Panzer Regiments zu schmälern.

Im August 1943 wurde Krag vorübergehend Kommandeur der Sturmgeschütz-abteilung, eine Ernennung, die dauerhaft wurde, als die Ereignisse an der Front die Unterlagen in Berlin überholten. Walter Kniep kehrte nach Deutschland zurück und sollte wieder zur 17. SS-Pz.Grenadier-Division "Götz von Berlichingen" als erster Kommandeur ihrer Panzer-Abteilung versetzt werden.

Krag führte die Abteilung beim Kampf um den Brückenkopf bei Saporoshje und wurde am 14 Oktober 1943 nochmals verwundet. "Das Reich" setzte ihre Kämpfe Ende Oktober bis Mitte November 1943 entlang den Hauptstrassen in Richtung Kiew fort bis die Einheit in den Raum Korostyschew verlegt wurde, um sich auf die Kämpfe um Shitomir im Dezember vorzubereiten.

Trotz der schweren Verluste der Division, verteidigte sich die Abteilung gut, wie durch die Verleihung des Ritterkreuzes an einen von Krag's Batterieführern, Dr. Wolfgang Roehder, bestätigt wird. Als enger Freund von Krag und der jüngste Offizier, der ihn am meisten beeindruckte, sollte Roehder später auf Empfehlung von Krag die Abteilung übernehmen.[36]

Die Division brauchte eine vollständige Erholung und Neuausrüstung, und so wurde der größte Teil der Division nach Deutschland verlegt, um als Panzer-Division in Fallingbostel neu aufgestellt zu werden. Krag's Männer liessen ihre restlichen Sturmgeschütze mit der Kampfgruppe "Das Reich" zurück. Diese Kampfgruppe wurde in 2 Kompanien zusammengefaßt und von SS-Haupt-sturmführer Hans-Joachim Mützelfeld geführt.[37] Im März und April 1944 kehrte die Kampfgruppe zur Division zurück.

Krag beaufsichtigte die Neuaufstellung der Sturmgeschützabteilung Anfang 1944 und wurde am 20. Februar 1944 offiziell ihr Kommandeur.[38] Er sollte die Abteilung gegen die Alliierten nach der Invasion nur für kurze Zeit führen bis er Kommandeur der Aufklärungsabteilung wurde, die ebenfalls nach schweren Verlusten wieder neu aufgestellt worden war. Auf Antrag des Divisions-Kommandeurs, SS-Brigadeführer Heinz Lammerding, wurde Krag am 20 April 1944 zum SS-Sturmbannführer befördert.

Als "Das Reich" im Juni 1944 gegen die Alliierten eingesetzt wurde, ergaben sich ganz andere taktische Probleme als in Russland. Die dauernde Bedrohung aus der Luft hielt alle Bewegungen der Truppe auf ein Minimum beschränkt. Die Jagdbomber verursachten schwere Verluste während des gesamten Feldzuges. Der Mangel an Treibstoff und anderem Nachschub vergrößerte die Probleme bei allen Einheiten. Auch bei den Kampfhandlungen waren die Verluste schwer, und am 5. Juli 1944 wurde Krag bei den Kämpfen im Raum La Haye-du-Puits erneut verwundet.

Anfang Juli 1944 wurde auch der Kommandeur der Aufklärungsabteilung, SS-Hauptsturmführer Heinrich Wulf, verwundet.[39] Zwei Wochen später unterzeichnete Krag seinen letzten Vorschlag für das Deutsche Kreuz in Gold für einen seiner Zugführer, Roland Paul, der u.a. 37 Sowjetpanzer innerhalb von 6 Monaten im vorhergehenden Sommer vernichtet hatte. Eine Woche vor diesem Antrag, am 21. Juli 1944, hatte Krag mit Paul und seinen Männern und Teilen des Regiments "Deutschland" einen Angriff im Raum St. Loieferte geführt und 3 Sherman-Panzer abgeschossen.[40]

Dann trat Krag sein Kommando über die Sturmgeschützabteilung an SS-Hauptsturmführer Dr. Wolfgang Roehder ab und wurde der letzte Kommandeur der Aufklärungsabteilung.[41] Die Kämpfe in der Normandie waren von Anfang an schwer und viele Kommandeure wurden entweder verwundet oder fielen. Auch Heinz Lammerding wurde verwundet und durch den Kommandeur des Panzer-Regiments, Christian Tychsen, ersetzt.

---

36 Brief des Autors von Herrn Krag v. 19.11.1985.

37 Mützelfeld hatte die 3./Flak-Abteilung geführt, bei der er am 26.11.1943 das Deutsche Kreuz in Gold erhielt. Die verbliebenen Sturmgeschütze kämpften tapfer, wie durch die Verleihung des Deutschen Kreuzes in Gold an Untersturmführer Karl Gerlach (2.7.1944) und Hauptscharführer Gerhand Hecker (2.7.1944) für ihr Handeln in der gemischten Sturmgeschütz-Abteilung, die der Kampfgruppe angeschlossen war, bewiesen wird.

38 SS-Führungshauptamt V/Abt. IIa/Ref. 3, Az. 21c 16 Lg/Ge Stu.Gesch. "Personalverfügung".

39 Heinrich Wulf war Lehrer an der Junkerschule Bad Tölz ehe er zur Kampfgruppe "Das Reich" kam, wo er die gemischte Aufklärungskompanie führte. Lammerding schlug ihn für das Deutsche Kreuz in Gold vor. Wulf kehrte nach Deutschland zurück, um die Führung der Aufklärungsabteilung von SS-Hauptsturmführer Walter Drexler zu übernehmen, der wiederum die Teile der Einheit übernahm, die sich schon in der Neuaufstellung befanden. Wulf kam 1938 von der Junkerschule Braunschweig und wurde am 1. Januar 1945 zum SS-Sturmbannführer ernannt als er der Panzer-Aufklärungsabteilung angehörte.

40 "Vorschlag Nr. 4 für die Verleihung des Deutschen Kreuzes in Gold", datiert 21. Juli 1944 und unterzeichnet von Krag. Paul, einem Obersturmführer und Zugführer der 3. Batterie, wurde das "Deutsche Kreuz in Gold" am 28. August 1944 verliehen. Damals war das Regiment wieder mit der Sturmgeschützabteilung und Panzerjägerabteilung ergänzt worden, und so waren diese beiden Einheiten wieder vereinigt. Während die meisten Abt. Offiziere von der Sturmgeschützabteilung kamen, stellte den Großteil ihrer Waffen die Panzer-Jäger-Abteilung. Die Empfehlung fur Paul's Deutsches Kreuz in Gold ist mit dem Stempel der Sturmgeschütz-Abteilung versehen, während der Kopf des Dokuments die Pz.-Jäger-Abt. ausweist.

41 Unter den früheren Kommandeuren waren Dr. Wim Brandt (Erfinder der Tarnanzüge), Hans Mühlenkamp (späterer Eichenlaubträger bei "Wiking"), Wilhelm Kment (Deutsches Kreuz in Gold beim Kradschützen Bataillon "Das Reich"), Hans Weiss (Ritterkreuz bei SS-Pz.-Abt. 102), Otto Weidinger (Schwerter als Regiments-Kommandeur "Der Führer"), Jakob Fick (Ritterkreuz bei "Langemarck") und Heinrich Wulf (Siehe Fußnote 40).

Als ein amerikanischer gepanzerter Stosstrupp den Divisionsgefechtsstand an der Kreuzung von Trelly angriff, wurde Tychsen getötet. Er wurde am 28. Juli 1944 durch Otto Baum ersetzt.[42] Es sollte Baum sein, der Krag für das Ritterkreuz für seinen Einsatz im Raum um Coutance im späten Juli 1944 vorschlug.

Krag's neues Kommando bestand aus 4 Kampf-Kompanien und einer Begleitkompanie. Ausgerüstet mit verschiedenen 4- und 8-Rad gepanzerten Fahrzeugen sowie einem Halbkettenfahrzeug, war die Einheit oft an der Spitze der Division zu finden, wo sie sich dem Gegner mit einer überlegenen Feuerkraft entgegenstellte. Die Abteilung hatte auch den berühmten Schwimmwagen, der von Prof. Dr. Ferdinand Porsche entworfen war. Nachdem Krag das Kommando übernommen hatte, ergab sich für ihn und andere Einheiten die Notwendigkeit, sich aus dem Raum Coutance zu lösen. Für den Ausbruch sollte Krag's Aufklärungsabteilung zusammen mit Regiment "Deutschland" die Flanke der Division gegen kanadische Truppen verteidigen, die auf Granville vorstiessen.

"Als in der Nacht vom 28./29. Juli 1944 die 2.SS-Panzer-Division 'Das Reich' aus ihrer Umklammerung nordöstl. von Avranches nach Südwesten ausbrach, um eine neue Verteidigungslinie zwischen Percy und Souredevall aufzubauen, blockierte SS-Sturmbannführer Krag den bereits durchsickernden Feind in Gavray und verhinderte damit einen Angriff auf die offene Flanke der Division. Obwohl Krag sich seiner gefährdeten Lage bewusst war, entschied er in eigener Verantwortung und erreichte mit seinen schwachen Kräften einen vollen Abwehrerfolg über den überlegenen Feind. Durch diesen tapferen Einsatz, den SS-Sturmbannführer Krag mit seiner Abteilung führte, wurde es seiner Division und anderen Einheiten des LXXXIV.Korps ermöglicht, eine neue Verteidigungslinie aufzubauen. Krag vernichtete im Raum Gavray mit seiner Einheit 9 Feindpanzer und eine Anzahl gepanzerter und ungepanzerter Fahrzeuge, die für den Feind schwere Verluste bedeuteten". [43]

Nach diesen Gefechten kämpften Krag's Männer mit seiner früheren Sturmgeschützabteilung und Regiment "Deutschland" zusammen im Raum Mortain. Dann setzten sie sich auf Divisionsbefehl teilweise ab. Hier zeichnete sich bereits der Kessel von Falaise ab, wo die Alliierten eine große Zahl sich absetzender deutscher Kräfte im August 1944 einschlossen.

Am 26. Juli 1944 wurde Krag bei den Kämpfen um Coutance verwundet und erhielt das goldene Verwundetenabzeichen. Anfang August wurden ihm zwei weitere Auszeichnungen verliehen: das Panzer-Kampfabzeichen in Silber (2.8.44) und die Nahkampfspange in Silber (12.8.44). Diese Auszeichnungen erhielt er für eine bestimmte Anzahl Kampftage als Sturmgeschützabteilungs-und als Panzer-Aufklärungsabteilungs-Kommandeur verliehen.[44]

Während Krag mit seinen Männern im Raum Mortain kämpfte, versuchten die Alliierten ihn und auch andere Einheiten einzuschließen, indem sie den Raum südlich und südöstlich der Stadt besetzten. Sie hofften, Trun zu erobern, das von Krag's Einheit, II./"Der Führer" und der Sturmgeschützabteilung verteidigt wurde. Eine große Anzahl deutscher Truppen setzte sich bereits von dem sich bildenden Kessel ab als Krag mit seinen Männern den Feind nordöstl. der Stadt zum Kampf stellte.

Ihnen stand die 1. Polnische Division gegenüber. Krag's Männer mit Teilen der Sturmgeschützabteilung vernichteten 6 britische Panzer, ohne daß sie Artillerie-unterstützung erhielten und schlugen alle Angriffe zurück. Bei den eigenen Vorbereitungen, sich aus dem Kessel zurückzuziehen, erhielt Krag einen Befehl des II.SS-Panzer-Korps, diese Stellungen auf jeden Fall zu halten, auch dann, wenn er sich selbst mit seinen Männern nicht mehr absetzen könne. Dieser ausdrückliche Befehl war nötig, damit sich so viele Truppen wie möglich geordnet zurückziehen konnten. Dieser Befehl wurde durch Melder überbracht, da es keine andere Verbindung mehr mit dem Korps oder dem Rest der Division "Das Reich" aufgrund der Kampflage gab.

In dem Moment als Krag mit seinen Männern fast vollständig eingeschlossen war, befahl er den Ausbruch. Krag selbst übernahm das Kommando über die Infanterie, die die restlichen gepanzerten Fahrzeuge bei diesem Ausbruch deckte. Sie schlugen eine Bresche in den noch in Bewegung befindlichen Einschließungsring des Feindes und stießen auf Chambois vor. In dem totalen Durcheinander unter den anderen sich absetzenden Truppen, fand Paul Hausser seinen Weg zum Kommando der Aufklärungsabteilung. Obwohl verwundet und von Krag über die Lage aufgeklärt, setzte er seinen Weg zum nächsten Korps-Gefechtsstand fort, um bei der Zurücknahme der Truppen, die sich noch im Kessel befanden, Hilfe zu leisten.[45]

Weil Krag und seine Männer ihre Stellungen in Chambois hielten, konnten große Truppenteile dem alliierten Einschließungsring entkommen. Der Kommandeur der "Leibstandarte", SS-Brigadeführer "Teddy" Wisch, wurde von Krag's Männern gerettet, nachdem er mehrere Lungenschüsse erhalten hatte. Während des Rückzugs einer Panther-Einheit des Heeres, die sich Krag's Kommando unterstellte und seine Befehle ausführte, erhielt Krag Unterstützung bei

[42] Tychsen hatte Lammerding nach dessen Verwundung ersetzt. Nach Tychsen's Tod übernahm Baum die Division, während er gleichzeitig die 17. SS-Panzer-Grenadier-Division "Götz von Berlichingen" führte. Baum wurden am 2. September 1944 die Schwerter zum Ritterkreuz für die Führung der Division "Das Reich" verliehen. Lammerding kehrte am 1. Nov. 1944 zur Division zurück und Baum übernahm die 16.SS-Panzer-Grenadier-Division "Reichsführer SS".

[43] "Vorschlag Nr. 7 für die Verleihung des Ritterkreuzes zum Eisernen Kreuz", datiert 15. Sept. 1944. gezeichnet Otto Baum.

[44] Die erforderliche Anzahl Kampftage sind in Krag's Soldbuch bis Ende Januar 1945 eingetragen.

[45] "Bericht über Kessel Falaise/Einsatz AA bei Trun" von Ernst August Krag, 29.5.44.

der Verteidigung. Angesichts einer Übermacht alliierter Panzer- und Infanterie-Einheiten befahl der Kommandeur der Division "Das Reich", Otto Baum, sich nach Rouen abzusetzen, damit die Seine überschritten und eine sichere Frontlinie neu aufgebaut werden konnte. Krag's Männer, die unter dauerndem Feinddruck standen, kämpften sich mit Teilen des Regiments "Der Führer" unter dem Befehl von SS-Sturmbannführer Otto Weidinger zur Stadt Elbeuf durch.[46]

Der Raum um die Brücke von Rouen wurde von dem Kommandeur des Regiments "Deutschland", SS-Obersturmbannführer Günther Wisliceny, gehalten. Ehe die Aufklärungsabteilung mit Resten der Sturmgeschützabteilung den Fluß überschritten, verteidigten sie den Raum südlich der Brücke, so daß die anderen Einheiten der Division die Brücke überqueren konnten. Aufgrund der andauernden alliierten Luftangriffe, mußte die Brücke von Krag und seinen Männern bei Nacht überquert werden, was nur geringe Ausfälle zur Folge hatte. Durch den Einsatz des II./"Der Führer", der Sturmgeschützabteilung und Krag's Aufklärungsabteilung konnte ein grosser Teil der Truppen für einen späteren Kampfeinsatz gerettet werden. Diese Einheiten, die überlegenen alliierten Kräften erfolgreich Widerstand leisteten, gaben trotz der sich anbahnenden Panik anderer sich absetzender Truppenteile, ein wahres Beispiel an Tapferkeit und Disziplin gegen eine überwältigende Übermacht. Obwohl in der Geschichte der Waffen-SS der offensive Erfolg unterstrichen wird, war es die Stärke bei Abwehrkämpfen, die zahlreiche kritische Situationen in den letzten beiden Kriegsjahren rettete.

Krag führte seine Männer in Richtung belgische Grenze, wo der Aufklärungsabteilung bei Wassigny der Treibstoff ausging und ihre Stellung durch feindliche Panzer-Einheiten überrollt wurde. In ähnlichen Situationen hatte man die Einheit als gefangengenommen angesehen und den nachfolgenden Truppen überlassen. Krag jedoch akzeptierte diese Situation nicht und schickte einen Spähtrupp aus, um nach Treibstoff zu suchen. Nachdem sie einen Wagen mit genug Benzin für eine 120-Kilometer-Fahrt beladen hatten, nahmen sie diesen ins Schlepp und tankten damit ihre leeren Fahrzeuge wieder auf.

Dann brachen Krag und seine Männer aus den Stellungen hinter den Feindlinien auf und stellten die Verbindung mit dem Rest der Division wieder her, um sich weiter kämpfend in Richtung Westwall abzusetzen. Dabei verloren sie nur 2 Halbkettenfahrzeuge. In Oisy stellten sie sich wieder zum Kampf.[47] Am 15. September 1944 beantragte Otto Baum das Ritterkreuz für Krag, das am 23. Oktober 1944 genehmigt wurde. Der Divisionskommandeur, SS-Brigadeführer Heinz Lammerding, überreichte Krag im November 1944 vor der versammelten Aufklärungsabteilung in einer Feierstunde in Borgentreich[48] die Auszeichnung.

Als Krag's Abteilung in ihrer Stellung im Westwall abgelöst wurde, um bei Mayen mit dem Rest der Division neu aufgestellt zu werden, betrug die Gesamtstärke nur noch etwas über 100 Mann. Nach schneller Aufrüstung war die Aufklärungsabteilung in der Ardennenoffensive Mitte Dezember 1944 im Einsatz. Bei dieser letzten deutschen Offensive im Westen war Krag als Abteilungskommandeur der Aufklärungsabteilung der höchstdekorierte Offizier der Aufklärungsabteilung.[49]

Obwohl Betriebsstoffmangel herrschte, war Krag's Abteilung wieder zu beträchtlicher Kampfstärke für die bevorstehende Offensive aufgefrischt worden. Zu den vier Kompanien kamen Halbketten- und Räderfahrzeuge für die Infanterie sowohl mit 2 cm als auch mit 7.5 cm Kanonen bestückt. Die 4. Kompanie hatte auch einen Granatwerferzug, einen Pionierzug und eine PAK-Einheit. Bei der Eröffnung der Offensive führte Krag eine Kampfgruppe, die aus seiner Aufklärungsabteilung, 2./Sturmgeschützabteilung, I./Artillerie-Regiment, 1./Pionier-Bataillon und einem Sanitätszug bestand.[50]

Ihre ursprüngliche Aufgabe war es, taktische Aufklärung im Raum Joubival durchzuführen. Kurz vorm Ziel des Auftrages entfernt, erhielten die Spitzen in der Stadt Ottre intensives Artilleriefeuer. Krag hatte seinen Gefechtsstand in der Stadt und musste mehrere Stunden ununterbrochenes schweres Artilleriefeuer überstehen bis die Stadt völlig in Flammen stand. Aufgrund der eingetretenen Verluste konnte der Angriff auf Joubival nicht weitergeführt werden. Krag's Männer verteidigten Ottre gegen die Einnahme der Stadt durch den Feind und setzten sich gegen die alliierten Luftangriffe zur Wehr. Hierbei wurde Mitte Dezember ein feindlicher Aufklärungstrupp gefangengenommen. Ebenfalls konnten bei diesen Kämpfen viele überraschte alliierte Einheiten durch Krag's Kommando gefangengenommen werden. Als nächstes wurde die Stadt Salm-Chateau mit Unterstützung des Artillerie-Regiments unter der Führung von SS-Standartenführer Karl Kreutz genommen. Das Wetter zeigte seine günstige Seite und so bekam Krag den Auftrag, nochmals in Richtung Joubival vorzustossen, was am Weihnachtsabend 1944 erfolgreich gelang. Am ersten

46 Weidinger wurde das Eichenlaub zum Ritterkreuz fur diese Kämpfe verliehen. Siehe "Otto Weidinger, Ritterkreuz mit Eichenlaub und Schwertern" von Mark C. Yerger, Seite 61.

47 "Kämpfe bei Wassigny" von Ernst August Krag, 29.5.1954.

48 Brief an den Autor von Herrn Krag, datiert am 30.9.1987.

49 Bei der Verleihung einer Auszeichnung an einen Offizier war dieser oft in einer anderen Stellung als zu der Zeit als die Auszeichnung genehmigt wurde, denn es war für die Kämpfe, für die die Auszeichnung vergeben wurde. Nach Genehmigung wies daher die Verleihungsurkunde oft die augenblickliche Stellung aus; daher sind Nachkriegstexte, was die Zugehörigkeit des Einzelnen hinsichtlich seiner Auszeichnungen betrifft, in gewissem Sinn irreführend. Nur Krag (Eichenlaub) und Otto Weidinger (Ritterkreuz) erhielten Deutschlands höchste Auszeichnung für Kämpfe mit der Aufklärungsabteilung. Als Beispiel steht im Fall Weidinger auf dem Dokument der Auszeichnung seine Verwendung als Kampftruppenführer (was er z.Z. der Genehmigung war), obwohl die Auszeichnung für Tapferkeit an der Front als Kommandeur der Aufklärungsabteilung verliehen wurde.

50 "Einsatz der 2. SS-Panzer-Division 'Das Reich' Aufklärungsabteilung während der Ardennenoffensive 1944/45" von Ernst August Krag, 29.5.1954.

Weihnachtstag nahm SS-Sturmbannführer Otto Weidinger's Regiment "Der Führer" die kleine Stadt Malempre ein. Für die Kämpfe in der folgenden Woche erhielt Ernst August Krag das Eichenlaub zum Ritterkreuz verliehen.

"Am 2.1.45 blockte Krag mit seiner Aufklärungsabteilung einen starken Feind- einbruch mit 22 Panzern östlich von Malempre ab. Dabei erlitt der Feind schwere Verluste. In erbitterten, schweren Kämpfen wurde ein Vorstoß über die Kreuzung Baraque de Fraiture verhindert. Dies war für die Fortführung des Kampfes von besonderer Bedeutung. Trotz beiderseitig offener Flanken blockte Krag einen nochmaligen schweren Vorstosß des Feindes am 4.1.45 ab, der schwere Verluste auf der Seite des Feindes verursachte. Bei einem wagemutig geführten Gegenangriff mit 8 Pionieren bereinigte Krag einen Feindeinbruch, so daß am Abend unsere Sperrposition wieder fest in unserer Hand war.

"Weil Krag, trotz Einschließungsgefahr, seine Stellung an der Kreuzung Baraque de Fraiture mit nur wenigen Männern und Waffen hielt, war es für unsere anderen Einheiten rechts und links möglich, sich abzusetzen, einen Stellungswechsel vorzunehmen, der dringend notwendig wurde, den Feind zum Umgruppieren zu zwingen und den Einbruch nach Südosten zu vereiteln." [51]

Divisionskommandeur Heinz Lammerding legte den obigen Bericht am 11. Januar 1945 vor, und nachdem er durch den Armee-Oberkommandierenden, SS-Oberst-Gruppenführer Sepp Dietrich, geprüft war, wurde die Verleihung des Eichenlaubs zum Ritterkreuz am 28. Februar 1945 genehmigt. Ernst August Krag war der 755. Soldat der Deutschen Wehrmacht, dem das Eichenlaub zum Ritterkreuz verliehen wurde. Es war das einzige Eichenlaub, das einem Angehörigen der Aufklärungsabteilung "Das Reich" für Kampfeinsätze verliehen wurde.

Bei den letzten Kämpfen im Westen waren die Verluste schwer, jedoch wurde "Das Reich" mit anderen wichtigen Einheiten für Einsätze im Osten schnell wieder aufgefrischt. Nachdem die Division Koblenz verlassen hatte, kam sie Mitte Februar in Ungarn an und wurde sofort im Raum Mihalyi eingesetzt. Ihr neuer Kommandeur war SS-Gruppenführer Werner Ostendorff. Er überreichte Ernst August Krag das Eichenlaub im Divisionsgefechtsstand "Das Reich".[52]

Die letzten Wochen des Kampfes im Osten müssen von ungewöhnlicher Heftigkeit gewesen sein. Der meiste Ersatz war schlecht ausgebildet und ausgerüstet. Daß diese Einheiten überhaupt überlebten, ist dem wenigen verbliebenen Kader zu verdanken. Krags Männer kämpften auf der Linie zwischen dem I. und II.SS-Panzerkorps in der Nähe von Kaloz, östlich des Balaton-Sees.

Im März begann die grosse Sowjet-Offensive und die schwachen Einheiten von Sepp Dietrich's 6.SS-Panzer-Armee waren zahlenmäßig weit unterlegen. Sie stiessen nach Westen als die Russen in Richtung Österreich angriffen. Krag und seine Manner sowie andere SS-Einheiten versuchten, unrealistische Befehle auszuführen und kämpften so bis zum bitteren Ende.

Es scheint als ein Wunder, dass überhaupt Soldaten überlebt haben, wenn man die Anzahl der Divisionen bedenkt, die ihnen gegenüber standen und ihren völligen Mangel an Waffen und Munition. Man kann in der Divisionsgeschichte nachlesen, daß das Überleben zur Priorität wurde. Als das Ende kam, versuchten alle Einheiten, sich - wenn möglich - bei den Westmächten in Gefangenschaft zu begeben.

Am 8. Mai 1945, dem Kapitulationstag, wurden auf Befehl Krags Waffen und Geräte unbrauchbar gemacht und angeordnet, daß sich alle Angehörigen der Abteilung in kleinen Gruppen durch die bereits von Russen besetzten und von Tschechen kontrollierten Gebiete bis zu den englisch/amerikanischen Truppen durchschlagen. Dieses abenteuerliche Vorhaben ist nahezu gelungen. Daran anschliessend begann ein leidvoller, oft langer Weg in englisch/amerikanische Kriegsgefangenschaft.

Wie viele Soldaten der Waffen-SS, war auch Krag längere Zeit in Gefangenschaft und kehrte erst endgültig am 30.Januar 1948 nach Hause zurück. Und wie alle Soldaten der Waffen-SS, erhielt auch er keine Rente, wie sie den Soldaten des Heeres, der Marine und der Luftwaffe zugesprochen wurde. Der Gedanke, daß ein Mann wie Krag, der 5 1/2 Jahre an der Front gekämpft hat und 6 Mal verwundet wurde, kein Soldat im Sinne der rechtsgültigen Nachkriegsbürokratie sein soll, ist unlogisch und entspricht nicht den Tatsachen. Diese Art der kollektiven Beurteilung ist nicht der Weg, um eine Demokratie aufzubauen.

Da Krag keine vernünftige Arbeit im Nachkriegsdeutschland finden konnte, wurde er Bauingenieur und arbeitete in dieser Position bei Hilton in Istanbul. Nach Fertigstellung des Hotels kehrte er in seine deutsche Firma zurück und war dort bis zu seiner Pensionierung u.a. als Betriebsleiter tätig.

Ernst August Krag ist einer der ältesten Mitglieder der Ordensgemeinschaft der Ritterkreuzträger e.V. und betätigt sich hierin sowie auch in den Kameradschaften seiner alten Divison aktiv. 1988 schrieb er ein Buch über die Geschichte der Aufklärungsabteilung der Waffen-SS "An der Spitze". Nachdem er 5 Jahre ehrenhaft für sein Vaterland gekämpft und gelitten hatte, lebte er bis zu seinem Tod im Jahre 1994 mit seiner Frau Luise im Ruhestand. Außer seiner Frau hinterläßt er zwei Kinder und vier Enkel.

---

51 "Vorschlag für die Verleihung des Eichenlaubs zum Ritterkreuz des Eisernen Kreuzes", datiert v. 11.1.45 und unterzeichnet von Heinz Lammerding und Sepp Dietrich.

52 Brief an den Autor von Herrn Krag v. 30 Sept. 1987.

NACHWORT

Es war allein der Wunsch des amerikanischen Historikers Mark C. Yerger meinen soldatischen Werdegang in einer Biografie niederschreiben zu dürfen. Nachdem ich mich hinreichend überzeugt hatte, daß es Herrn Yerger's Absicht ist, vorurteilsfrei und realistisch zu schreiben, habe ich dem zugestimmt.

Als Unterlagen sind ausschließlich in Archiven lagernde amtliche Dokumente und zu deren Ergänzung authentisch belegbare Aufzeichnungen, Berichte und Photos verwendet worden.

Der Wahrheit wegen liegt mir sehr daran, besonders herauszustellen, dass die in der Biografie beschriebenen Einsätze nur durch grösstmöglichen tapferen Zusammenhalt aller daran beteiligten Kameraden erfolgversprechend durchgeführt werden konnten.

Es ist leidvoll und höchst bedauerlich, daß nicht wenige Kameraden, zumeist im blutjungen Alter, dabei ihr Leben verloren haben. Bei uns, den Überlebenden, werden diese treuen Kameraden und Mitstreiter, die letztlich auch für uns ihr Leben einsetzten, nicht vergessen werden.

Ihr Opfertod ist für uns Mahnung und Verpflichtung zugleich. Daß diesen Männer, teilweise von amtlichen Gremien, Achtung und Ehrerbietung versagt werden, ist eine beschämende Würdelosigkeit und kaum zu überbieten. Für dieses schändliche Verhalten gibt es keine moralisch stichhaltige Begründung.

Ernst August Krag
Niedernhausen
1994